The Spiritual Philosophy of the Tao Te Ching

Joseph A. Magno, Ph.D.

The Spiritual Philosophy of the Tao Te Ching

ISBN 1-932965-03-3
Library of Congress Cataloging-in-Publication Data

Magno, Joseph A., 1942-
The spiritual philosophy of the Tao te ching / Joseph A. Magno.
p. cm.
Includes bibliographical references and index.
ISBN 1-932965-03-3 (pbk.)
1. Laozi. Dao de jing. I. Title.

BL1900.L35M35 2004
299.5'1482--dc22

2004018115

Book design and typography by Crocker Design Company
Printed in the United States of America
Pendragon Publishing, Inc.
PO Box 31665
Chicago, IL 60631

To my Mother and Father

About the Author

Dr. Joe Magno is a member of the philosophy department at Loras College, Dubuque, IA. His primary areas of study include Eastern philosophy, philosophy of religion, philosophy of love, and philosophy of healing. Concerning the latter, he developed and has been practicing for over sixteen years a counseling method, "Self-acceptance Counseling," the main thrust of which is the recovery of self-love, and thereby, greater physical, psychological, relational, and spiritual wholeness, through the releasing of fears, *the* block to self-love.

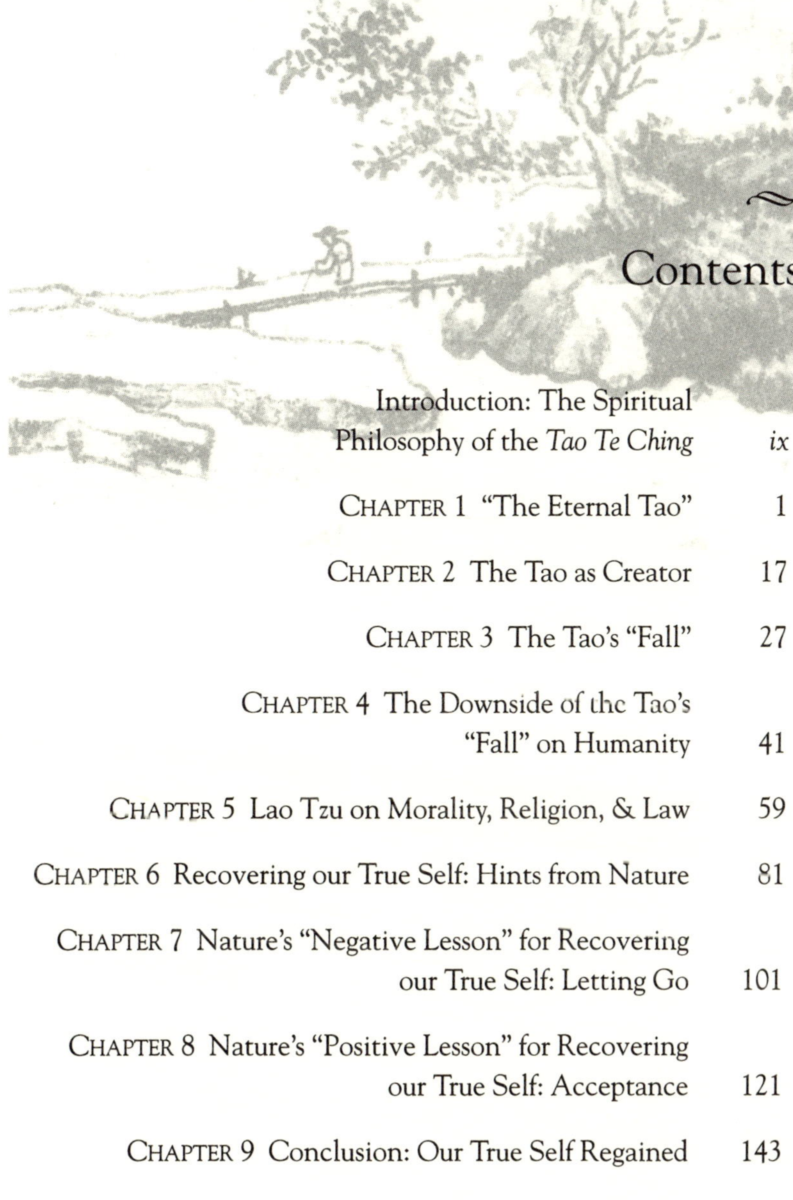

Contents

INTRODUCTION

The Spiritual Philosophy of the *Tao Te Ching*

Introduction to the Introduction

At the dawn of the first century BCE, Ssu-ma Ch'ien, author of the first known general history of China, the *Shih Chi (Records of Historians)*, devoted Chapter 63 to a brief biography of the sage, Lao Tzu (6th century BCE). The biography is brief because, as Ssu-ma Ch'ien candidly admits, he is both perplexed and amazed at just how little there is to report about Lao Tzu. Thus, of Lao Tzu all that the records reveal is that he was born in the village of Chu Jen (now the town of Luyi), in the area of Lai, the county of Hu, in the state of Chou; that his surname was Li, his proper name Erh, and his public name Tan; that Lao Tzu was therefore not Lao Tzu's actual name, but rather an honorific title bestowed upon him by his contemporaries, meaning the "Old Master"; that by profession he held the undistinguished position of court archivist of the Chou state; that at an old age, and tiring of his state's lack of spiritual understanding, he left Chou and traveled West, eventually reaching the pass in the mountain of Han-ku; that there he was recognized by the city's gatekeeper, Yin Hsi, who requested that he commit to writing his spiritual views before continuing on his journey; that Lao Tzu acceded to Yin Hsi's request, and, upon completing his book, the *Tao Te Ching*—consisting of approximately 5,350 words—resumed his westward trek, never to be seen or heard from again.[1]

Such is the sum and substance of historian Ssu-ma Ch'ien's account of the life and times of Lao Tzu, as well as of the origin of his book, the *Tao Te Ching*. What are we to make of this ancient historian's ever-so brief biographical sketch? The answer is that no one knows for sure. Which is to say, no one knows for sure how faithfully the scant information we possess about Lao Tzu portrays the Sage, or, for that matter, whether it actually portrays a Sage who once inhabited this mortal coil! Moreover, as to Ssu-ma Ch'ien's depiction of the origin of the *Tao Te Ching*, we know at least this much: that if indeed a flesh and blood man respectfully referred to as Lao Tzu penned said book some 2600 years ago, its original title was decidedly not the *Tao Te Ching*, but rather the *Lao Tzu*. Its current title,*Tao Te Ching*, was actually conferred upon the book at a much later date, somewhere between the first century BCE and the first century CE of the Han dynasty.[2]

Now, let me openly confess that, personally, and for reasons that exceed the scope of this book, I neither doubt the reality of Lao Tzu nor that he was the principal, if not sole, author of the book that was later to be dubbed the *Tao Te Ching*. But personal sentiments aside, whether Lao Tzu actually existed and authored the *Tao Te Ching* is, for the purposes of this book, at least, a moot point. For whoever its author or authors may have been,[3] the plain fact remains that the *Tao Te Ching* has been the subject of more than 1,000 commentaries and over forty translations in English alone (following closely behind only the Bible and the works of Shakespeare.) The indisputable point, then, is that this Classic has long exerted a profound influence well beyond the borders of China itself, an influence further evidenced by the spate of Tao of... books currently in print, including *The Tao of Physics*, *The Tao of Coaching*, *The Tao of Negotiation*, *The Tao of Management*, and even *The Tao of Cleaning* and *The Tao of Pooh!*[4]

So influential a book attests to the quality of its message, which message we may initially glean from its title, the *Tao Te Ching*, where *Ching* means Book, and more exactly, a *Classic* Book; Tao signifies Way, and in two primary senses: first, as the formless, eternal, infinite, and ineffable Source of all that is, and second, as a way of life in keeping with the Tao-given natural order that leads to reidentification with the "eternal Tao"; and Te generally stands for either Power or Virtue, and less generally for *true* Power, namely, the Power one experiences in consequence of one's communion with the Tao, and which manifests as intuitive spontaneity, effortlessness, allowing events to take their natural course, and unflappable inner peace. In short, literally taken, the *Tao Te Ching* translates to *The Classic of the Way and the Power.*[5]

Still, if this translation is indicative of the *Tao Te Ching's* overall message, it doubtless generates more questions than it answers. Accordingly, in an effort to resolve some of these unanswered questions and gain thereby a fuller appreciation of the book's fundamental message, let me propose that, in the final rendering, the *Tao Te Ching* is preeminently a work of spiritual philosophy. But this admittedly large claim warrants an explanatory word or two. So, permit me to explain, beginning with my contention that the *Tao Te Ching* is a work of spiritual philosophy.

The Spirituality of the *Tao Te Ching*

In maintaining that the *Tao Te Ching* is essentially a *spirituality*, my implied contention is that it is not, properly speaking, a religious work. In other words, it is a mistake to confuse, as frequently happens, the *Tao Te Ching* with Taoism as an organized religion. As an organized religion, Taoism, as Martin Palmer explains, is the product of "three main [converging] streams" of influence, the first of which is "shamanism" (the belief that there exists a physical world and a spiritual world "which the forces which guide and control the physical world inhabit," and to which the shaman has salutary access) "and the *fang-shih*" (officials "responsible for exorcisms ... medicine, divination, and other such practices.") The second stream of influence is "Lao Tzu and the schools of Chuang Tzu, etc.,"[6] with the third being "the quest for immortality" as a personal and not merely ancestral or communal quest. It is only when these "three main streams come together," concludes Palmer, "that we can really talk about there being such a thing as [religious] 'Taoism'."[7]

At most, we can say that certain of these "streams" that combined to beget religious Taoism, influenced the overall message of the *Tao Te*

Ching. For, as Palmer further notes, Lao Tzu and other early writers

> ... drew upon traditions and ideas which were current at the time, ideas which were held in common with Confucians, with Shamans, with practitioners of the cult of immortality. *However, there gradually evolved over the centuries, a faith, described by its contemporaries as 'Taoism', in which the philosophical and shamanistic, along with other influences came together.*[8] (Emphasis added)

Then too, and aside from the above, let's call it, historic reason for not according the *Tao Te Ching* a religious status, there are at least two good further reasons for not doing so. One is the patent fact that the *Tao Te Ching* regards religion, law, and morality as ultimately inadequate but temporarily useful sources of discipline, guidance, comfort, and hope, as long as "the great Tao is forgotten" (Poem 18), as long, that is, as we cleave to the illusory belief that we exist in separation from the Tao. As Lao Tzu holds religion in such 'provisional' regard, it seems highly unlikely that he would be of a mind to compose a foursquare religious book.

But that Lao Tzu did not intend to write a religious book becomes even more apparent when we consider the defining features of organized religion, to wit, adherence to a common core of beliefs, symbols, rituals, traditions, and ethical principles, as well as allegiance to an authority figure or figures and/or structure, all issuing in part or *in toto* from a divinely revealed Source, to which obedience and worship are due, and upon which one's salvation depends. If this is what religion essentially consists of, then the *Tao Te Ching* does not fit the bill as a religious work. For now, and until such time as I can offer more detailed evidence as to the "non-religious" character of the *Tao Te Ching* (in the subsequent chapters) I would but briefly indicate how this work differs in regards to what are undoubtedly the three most essential features of religion.

In the first place, conspicuously absent from the *Tao Te Ching* is the belief that our "salvation" necessarily requires faithful allegiance to an authority figure or figures and/or structure. That is, in vain do we search this work for prescribed "structures," e.g., liturgies, rituals, traditions, ceremonies, sacraments. The closest we come to anything resembling such "structures" are references to meditative practices and a way of life that is conducive to reunion with the Tao (see Chapter 8). Nor do we find in this work any support for the view that our salvation is entirely beholden to intercessory authority figures between ourselves and the divine, e.g., priests, ministers, rabbis, mullahs, vicarious saviors, and/or that our salvation requires us to submit, in faith, to personally non-demonstrable divine revelations, e.g., the doctrines of the Trinity, Incarnation, Resurrection. As to faith, this the *Tao Te Ching* rather regards as the decision to temporarily suspend judgment concerning the veracity of claimed spiritual truths until such time as one can personally, experientially verify said principles (see, for example, Poem 21). As to salvation hinging on intercessory figures between ourselves and the divine, this the *Tao Te Ching* rejects in light of its view that, as human nature is a naturally loving, immanent expression of the Tao, we possess the inherent capacity to liberate ourselves, and in fact, must so liberate ourselves (see Chapters 7 and 8).

In the second place, while Lao Tzu is in agreement with organized religion to the extent that he refers to the antiquity of his teachings (see Poems 15, 65), and even states that his teachings are "older than the world" (Poem 70), he nonetheless makes no claim that they are the product of a sacred, revealed text and/or founder. Rather, he holds that his teachings are "written in human beings' hearts" (Poem 32), and so, are accessible to anyone who "looks inside her heart." (Poem 70)[9]

Finally, whereas organized religion stresses a common path, in that it requires adherence to common beliefs, symbols, rituals, traditions, in short, common religious experiences, as necessary for salvation, the *Tao Te Ching* stresses the personal, in many ways unique, character of an individual's quest after reunion with the Tao:

> Use your own light
> and return to the source of light.
> This is called practicing eternity. (Poem 52)

And,

> When people no longer trust themselves,
> they begin to depend upon authority. (Poem 72)

In short, and as far as Lao Tzu is concerned, an individual (1) has direct access to the Tao, (2) possesses the inherent capacity to reunite with the Tao, and (3) must trust her own, in many ways unique, path, and hence, experiences, in her quest after reunion with the Tao.

Largely for the aforementioned reasons, then, I think we may confidently affirm that the *Tao Te Ching* does not belong to the literary genre, 'religious book'. Which brings us to my contention that the *Tao Te Ching* is better placed as a '*spiritual* book'. "Better placed," I say, because, while religion and spirituality are still often used interchangeably, since the 1980s, there has been a growing tendency to distinguish the one from the other, as in "I'm spiritual, not religious." For, whereas, and as was seen, religion essentially entails a common path, allegiance to intercessory authority figures and/or structures, and a divinely revealed Source as indispensable for salvation, spirituality, as conceived by many today, essentially upholds the uniqueness of each individual's path to union with the Source, the inherent capacity of each individual to experience union with the Source, and the necessity of trusting one's own, often highly personal, experiences to this unifying end.[10] But these essential marks of modern-day spirituality are the selfsame as those that essentially mark the spirituality of the *Tao Te Ching*, as was noted in the preceding paragraph. Whence, my claim that the *Tao Te Ching* is a *spiritual* book, a claim that, I believe, the forthcoming chapters will more fully justify.

The Philosophy of the *Tao Te Ching*

At the same time, and as was also indicated above, I am no less convinced that the *Tao Te Ching* equally qualifies as a *philosophic* book. This claim may seem quite a stretch, even for those prepared to grant the spiritual status of this work. And at first glance, there does appear to be more than sufficient grounds for questioning such a claim. Indeed, anyone at all familiar with this Chinese Classic cannot but be struck by the fact that, however insightful and profound its individual poems may be, taken as a whole, they present a seemingly random melange of insights and profundities.[11] And if one of the hallmarks of philosophy is a consistently reasoned argument in behalf of a given hypothesis, then, clearly, the *Tao Te Ching* doesn't pass muster as a philosophic work.

And yet, that there might be something to the claimed philosophic status of the *Tao Te Ching*, after all, it is worth noting that, historically, the book has been typically classified as a prime representative of "Taoist philosophy."[12] Assuming that there is some basis for this age-old classification, what might it be? I submit that while the book doesn't present an expressly systematic philosophy, it does nonetheless present an *implicitly* systematic philosophy. In which regard you might favorably compare the *Tao Te Ching* to an unassembled puzzle. For, like an unassembled puzzle, its pieces (statements, stanzas, Poems) only appear to be unrelated, whereas, upon closer inspection and with the investment of a good deal of time and effort, these seemingly unrelated pieces prove to fit harmoniously together to create a coherent picture or design (the statements, stanzas, and Poems cohering to produce a systematic philosophy.)

But in more exact, less analogical, terms, what does it mean to assert that the *Tao Te Ching* offers an implicitly systematic philosophy? It means, in the first place, that, appearances notwithstanding, and if we are prepared to unearth and piece together both the work's express and implied views, we will discover that it provides a consistently reasoned answer to three interconnected, ultimate questions: What is the origin of reality? What is the nature of reality? and What is the overriding purpose of reality? In the second place, and following directly from these ultimate, largely abstract, considerations, the *Tao Te Ching* puts forth a philosophy of life that leads to happiness and fulfillment by maximizing one's inherent, Tao-given capacity to realize the paramount purpose of life, reunion with the Tao.

Put still otherwise, the *Tao Te Ching*, in proffering its answer to the aforementioned ultimate questions and proposing a philosophy of life conducive to reconnection with the Tao, proceeds according to what we may call an *exitus-reditus* scheme, that is, and stated broadly, a scheme wherein all reality, issuing from the Tao, eventually finds its way back to the Tao.

Stated less broadly, I present this scheme in nine chapters. Thus, in Chapter 1, I begin with a discussion of the Tao's principal attributes, especially Its formlessness, infinity, and perfection, proceed to an examination of how we can know the Tao in the normal, conceptual manner, and conclude by preliminarily broaching Lao Tzu's view that conceptual knowledge of the Tao must be superseded in favor of intuitive knowledge of the Tao. In Chapter 2, I consider the nature of the Tao's creative activity, the Tao's transcendent-immanent relation to creation, and creation's main implications, especially, if not exclusively, for human creation. These are: (1) that human nature is an immanent expression of the Tao, and therefore, that human nature's veritable "True Nature" (Poem 65) is divine, and, (2) because the Tao is Love Itself, and human nature is an immanent expression of the Tao, human nature must needs be naturally loving. Chapter 3 investigates the "quasi-downside" of the Tao's decision to create, to wit, the Tao's willful "Fall," Its "forgetfulness" of Its transcendent, all-perfect Nature, so that It might partake of dualism, and thereby Self-express Itself in and through Its myriad created forms. Two major questions resulting from this "Fall" motif are raised and discussed: How can the infinite and all-perfect Tao be reasonably said to "forget" Its formless, transcendent Nature? and, Why would the infinite and all-perfect Tao even want to create? In Chapter 4, the discussion shifts to the specific bearing the Tao's willful "Fall" has on humanity. Which is primarily the necessity of overcoming dualism, the illusory belief that we are separate from the Tao, as well as all else, which, in its turn, begets attachment (fear-based desire) that is itself the proximate cause of humankind's three cardinal afflictions, "confusion," "sorrow," and a dearth of inner peace. Moreover, in view of the amount and degree of confusion and sorrow, in a word, suffering, occasioned by the Tao's decision to create, and hence to experience Itself in and through Its manifold forms (the Tao's "Fall"), raised and discussed is the question: Is the Tao's decision to create worth it? Chapter 5 treats of Lao Tzu's rejection of religion, morality, and law as ultimate answers to the attachment-born confusion, sorrow, and want of inner peace that, in their multitudinous ways, plague humankind. Religion, morality, and law are actually, Lao Tzu maintains, the products of our "forgetfulness" of our naturally loving Tao-Nature due to the "Fall"—which is to say, due to the illusory belief that our Nature is radically distinct from the Tao That is Love Itself. As such, religion, morality, and law are powerless to effect a reconnection with the Tao and thereby, the recovery of our naturally loving Nature. This reconnection and recovery can only be achieved by overcoming the main result of dualism, attachment. In so doing, we conquer attachment's main progeny, confusion, sorrow, and a lack of inner peace, recover our naturally loving Nature by dint of realizing a state of loving communion/reunion with the Tao That is Love, and for good measure, experience an intuitive connection with the Tao, whereby we spontaneously and immediately know what is the most loving course of action to take in a given situation. Chapter 6 commences Lao Tzu's prescriptions for conquering attachment toward the recovery of our True, Tao-Nature. In keeping with spiritual sages, past and present, he endorses the practice of meditation to this recovering end. However, along with this more traditional, meditative approach, he holds that, because the natural order is the purest manifestation of the immanent Tao, if we ponder the workings of nature we will discern a way of life perfectly suited to reconnecting with the Tao and, in the bargain, recovering our True Nature. After considering various passages suggestive of nature's lessons for recovering our True Nature, I note that these boil down to two interrelated, basic lessons, one "negative," the other "positive." The "negative lesson," letting go of control, I take up in Chapter 7 by way of passages illustrative both of Lao Tzu's general rejection of control (in that it is rooted in fear-based attachment) and of his rejection of specific modes of control. I style this lesson "negative" because, while it certainly points out the necessity of relinquishing control by overcoming attachment, it leaves undisclosed the specific way in which we are to go about overcoming attachment. Chapter 8 treats of nature's "positive lesson" for recovering our True

Nature, in that it specifically indicates the way in which we are to go about surmounting attachment to this Self-recovering end. This specific way is the way of acceptance, and in particular, self-acceptance, and for the following reasons. Detachment, the polar opposite of and antidote to attachment, is shown to be practically synonymous with self-acceptance, which is itself synonymous with self-love. And as love is the opposite of and antidote to fear, and fear is the main defining feature of attachment (*fear-based* desire), the practice of detachment, alias self-acceptance, alias self-love—the details of which practice I therein spell out—becomes, for Lao Tzu, the "natural" way of life that overcomes dualistically begotten, *fear-based* attachment, and insofar, leads to the recovery of our naturally loving Nature through reconnection with the Tao That *is* Love. Finally, in Chapter 9, I complete Lao Tzu's *exitus-reditus* cycle by discussing the life and times of the spiritual Master, the person who has achieved the pinnacle of spiritual success, the regaining of her True, Tao-Nature by virtue of her reunion with the Tao. More to the point, in this concluding chapter, I present in a summary manner the *Tao Te Ching's* take, first, on the principal attributes distinctive of the Master (which in the preceding chapters were presented in a less coherent manner), and then on what I term the Master's "cosmic" Influence both on the natural order, in general, and the human race, in particular.

Final Introductory Remarks

Before taking leave of this rather long-winded Introduction, three short further remarks are in order. The first is that throughout the first four chapters I often refer to the renowned medieval philosopher-theologian, Thomas Aquinas (1225–1274). I have chosen to do so, on the one hand, because Aquinas's insights into how we can talk meaningfully about a formless, infinite God are, I believe, equally relevant to Lao Tzu's implied question (in the first verse of Poem 1) as to how we can meaningfully talk about "the eternal Tao" that cannot "be told." Then too, I have elected to cite Aquinas because I thought it would be interesting as well as instructive (especially in this more globally conscious day-and-age) to compare and contrast this extraordinarily influential Western thinker's views with those of Lao Tzu on such further perennial issues as the nature and attributes of the Source, the Source's act of Creation, the Source's transcendent-immanent relation to creation, the Source's "Fall", why the infinite, all-perfect Source elects to create, and, in view of the amount of pain and suffering wrought by creation, whether the Source's decision to create is really worth all the fuss!

My second (succinct) point has to do with something the Reader may have observed in the foregoing paragraphs, namely, my referring to the eighty-one sections that comprise the *Tao Te Ching* as "poems." To be sure, I am not the first to do so, so that there is a precedent for so doing.[13] Even so, given my efforts to convince that the *Tao Te Ching* is a book of spiritual *philosophy*, my further claim that this great Classic equally qualifies as a book of poetic philosophy may seem a tad far-fetched. But that this may not be too far-fetched a claim, after all, I would simply note that, while philosophy and poetry certainly constitute different literary genres, they are not, for all that, necessarily incompatible genres. A case in point: the very *Tao Te Ching!* For, if poetry amounts to a verbal composition meant to convey ideas, experiences, and emotions in an imaginative manner, marked by the use of suggestively condensed language, as well as by the use of such literary devices as metaphor, irony, and paradox; if this, as I say, fairly characterizes poetry, then the *Tao Te Ching*, as I believe the ensuing chapters will bear out, passes muster as a work of poetic philosophy, as well as a work of spiritual philosophy.

The final point has to do with my choice of translation. As noted above, there exist more than forty translations of the *Tao Te Ching* in English alone. And while most of these translations are excellent and worthy of adoption, I have seen fit to adopt that of Dr. Stephen Mitchell,[14] and for two principal reasons. The first is that, in my opinion, Dr. Mitchell manages, more than any translator of which I am aware, to strike the delicate interpretive balance between modernity and antiquity, by utilizing symbols, metaphors, images, and examples that are meaningfully relevant to our own time, culture, and context, without sacrificing or compromising the overall integrity, meaning, and message of this great work. No small feat! My second reason for adopting Dr. Mitchell's translation is my conviction that he, again more than any translator of which I am aware, captures *the* message of the *Tao Te Ching*, namely, that acceptance, and in particular, *self*-acceptance, is the true "philosopher's stone" and spiritual "pearl of great price," the long-forgotten, neglected, and commonly rejected key to recovering our True, Tao-Nature. Again, no small feat!

So much for the how and why of the *Spiritual Philosophy of the Tao Te Ching*. I now invite you to explore with me this spiritual philosophy in the ensuing chapters, beginning, in Chapter 1, with the most fundamental of all spiritual questions: How can we talk about "the eternal Tao" that Lao Tzu insists is beyond what we can talk about?

Notes

1. The details of Lao Tzu's life, such as they are, may be gleaned from numerous studies of Taoism, of which I would recommend Holmes Welch's account of "The Problem of Lao Tzu," in his *Taoism: The Parting of the Way* (USA: Beacon Press, 1957), pp. 1–17. For an interesting discussion of the possible symbolism surrounding the book's reputed origin, see Martin Palmer, *The Elements of Taoism* (MA: Element Inc, 1991), pp. 36–37.

2. See D.C. Lau's "Introduction" to his translation of Lao Tzu's *Tao Te Ching* (NY: Penguin Books, 1963), pp. 7–8.

3. See Palmer, *The Elements of Taoism*, pp. 37–38.

4. Fritjof Capra, *The Tao of Physics*, 2nd edition (Boston: Shambhala, 1983); Max Landsberg, *The Tao of Coaching* (Knowledge Exchange, 1997); Joel Edelman and Mary Beth Crain, *The Tao of Negotiation* (NY: HarperPerennial, 1994); Bob Messing, *The Tao of Management* (Atlanta, GA: Humanics Pub Group, 1988); A. W. Ku, *The Tao of Cleaning* (Box Turtle Press, 1997); Benjamin Hoff, *The Tao of Pooh* (NY: Penguin Books, 1982.

5. See Palmer, *The Elements of Taoism*, pp. 39–40. Variations on this more literal title include the *Tao Te Ching*, *The Way of Life*, *The Way of the Tao Te Ching*, *The Tao Teh King*, and *The Tao of the Tao Te Ching*.

6. Along with the *Tao Te Ching*, two other notable books composed during

the classic period of Taoism (700–220 BCE) are the *Chuang Tzu* and the *Lieh Tzu*, named after their reputed authors, Chuang Tzu and Lieh Tzu, respectively.

7. Palmer, *The Elements of Taoism*, pp. 14, 20, 73. Also see Welch, *Taoism: The Parting of the Way*, pp. 88–90.

8. Palmer, *Ibid.*, p. 21. As to the time period in which Taoism developed into a religion, Eva Wong writes: "If the periods known as Spring and Autumn and the Warring States [700–220 BCE] were the golden age of Taoist philosophy, then the era between the beginning of the Eastern Han dynasty (25–219 CE) and the end of the Southern and Northern dynasties (304–589 CE) was the golden age of Taoist religion. During this era, Taoism became an organized religion, instituted a priesthood, developed a set of sacred ceremonies and scriptures, and acquired a large number of followers." Eva Wong, *The Shambhala Guide to Taoism* (Boston: Shambhala, 1997), p. 31. For a succinct statement of the development of Taoism into an organized religion, see Joel Kupperman, *Classic Asian Philosophy* (NY: Oxford University Press, Inc., 2001), p.112.

9. By contrast, as John Blofeld explains, "The [religious] Taoists like to refer to their system of belief as 'Huang Lao', thus honouring Huang Ti (the Yellow Emperor [claimed to have reigned from 2697–2597 BCE]) and Lao Tzu as their founders." *Taoism: The Road to Immortality* (Boston: Shambhala, 1978), p. vi.

10. For an excellent study of spirituality vis-à-vis religion, I recommend Marilyn Ferguson's book, *The Aquarian Conspiracy* (Los Angeles, CA: J.P. Tarcher, Inc., 1980), especially Chapter 11.

11. Palmer articulates the seemingly non-philosophical character of the *Tao Te Ching* as follows: "As a book, it falls into a category of ancient literature ... that uses short, pithy statements which are obviously meant to stand on their own—that is, there is usually no clear link with what comes next." *The Elements of Taoism*, p. 40.

12. See Isabelle Robinet, *Taoism: Growth of a Religion*, trans. Phyllis Brooks (Stanford, CA: Stanford University Press, 1997), pp. 25–41.

13. For example, at least as far back as 1955, R. B. Blakney, in the "Introduction" to his translation of the *Tao Te Ching*, which he entitles *The Way of Life* (NY: Mentor Books, 1955), p. 26, saw fit to so refer to the *Tao Te Ching's* eighty-one sections as "poems."

14. Lao Tzu, *Tao Te Ching*, 2nd edition, trans. Stephen Mitchell (NY: Perennial Classics, 2000).

CHAPTER ONE

"The Eternal Tao"

Those who know don't talk.
Those who talk don't know.

Lao Tzu, Tao Te Ching, Poem 56

Introduction

> The Tao that can be told is not the eternal Tao.[1]

So begins Lao Tzu's *Tao Te Ching*, and so too must our discussion of this ancient text begin. But no sooner do we undertake this discussion than Lao Tzu implicitly serves notice that any such discussion is ultimately beyond discussion! For, if the Tao about which we *can* speak is other than the "eternal Tao," the Tao as supreme and transcendent Reality, then how, pray, are we supposed to talk about that which we ultimately can't talk about? To be sure, it seems a foregone conclusion that any would-be discussion of the *Tao Te Ching* is doomed before we've even begun.

And yet, permit me to suggest that a discussion of the "eternal Tao" isn't the foredoomed undertaking that it would appear to be. As we shall soon see, to maintain, as indeed we must, that the Tao is beyond language, or, in more technical parlance, that the Tao is ineffable, does not thereby entail the conclusion that we can say nothing whatsoever about the Tao, and hence, that "Tao-talk" is utterly meaningless talk. But before proceeding to show how and why "Tao-talk," even granting its ineffability, admits of *some* talk, and hence, isn't sheer meaningless talk, we'll first need to determine what is at the bottom of Lao Tzu's conviction that the "eternal Tao" is perforce an *ineffable* Reality.

The Tao as "Formless"

That the Tao is, and can only be, an ineffable Reality Lao Tzu makes (obliquely) clear in Poem 25, wherein he writes,

> There was something formless and perfect
> before the universe was born,

which,

> For lack of a better name,
> I call it the Tao.

What are we to make of Lao Tzu's depiction of the Tao as, first and foremost, a "formless" Reality? Well, to speak of the Tao as formless means just what it says: that, in Its own fundamental Nature, the Tao, unlike all else, is non-composed, has no internal "parts," and admits of no inner distinguishing features, properties, or classifications![2]

Mythic Formlessness: The Source as "Chaos"

If you find the Tao's inherent "formlessness" a less than fathomable view, you're in good company. But so as to render this view less unfathomable, I would first call your attention to the fact that this very "formless" view has been poetically, figuratively, and metaphorically adumbrated in virtually all of the world's great creation myths. Indeed, a survey of Mesopotamian, Egyptian, Chinese, East Indian, Japanese,

African, Norse, Greek, Polynesian, and Native American creation myths reveals a common tendency to depict the cosmos, the created order, as being "born" of "the Abyss" or of "Chaos." Evidently, the assumption underlying each of these ancient myths is that, if the cosmos had a beginning, and if the cosmos *is* the created order, and thus implies a multiplicity and variety of unified forms, then the original "birthing" Source must needs be itself devoid of multiplicity, variety, and unified forms, and so, in the poetic parlance of the myths, "the Abyss" or, what amounts to the same thing, "Chaos." Put otherwise, through figurative means the myths are endeavoring to make sense of the cosmos itself. For, if the cosmos did have a beginning, then it must have been begotten by a Source other than the cosmos itself—if you will, an acosmic Source, which the myths figuratively portray as an "Abyss" or "Chaos."[3]

Nor is this primordial intuition and expression of the formlessness of the Source confined to sheer figurative and mythic representations. The great religions have no less endorsed this view, and have seen fit to do so in more formally explicit fashion. In which regard, consider two salient cases in point, the first from the Old Testament, the other from a man many believe to be *the* major Christian thinker.

Old Testament Formlessness: God as the "I Am"

Of all the mystery-laden stories that grace the pages of the Old Testament perhaps none is more mysterious than the Exodus 3 narrative of Moses encountering God on Mount Horeb. The story goes as follows. While tending his father-in-law's flock, Moses leads them to Mount Horeb, where he witnesses a burning bush that "was not being burned up." Intrigued by this strange phenomenon, and wishing to take a closer look, Moses approaches the bush, only to hear God call his name and admonish him not to venture too near to "holy ground." After recovering from the shock of this encounter, Moses receives an even bigger shock: God informs Moses that He has handpicked him to lead His people, the Israelites, out of bondage to the Egyptians and into the promised land. Downing his considerable misgivings and self-doubts, and reluctantly accepting his God-bestowed mission, Moses, before taking leave of God, asks God a seemingly natural question: "If they ask me what his [your] name is, what am I to tell them?" To which inquiry after His proper name God responds: "I Am who I Am. This ... is what you must say to the sons of Israel: 'I Am has sent me to you.'" (Exodus 3:1-14; The Jerusalem Bible)

What exactly has God revealed to Moses as to His proper name? Precisely that God has no proper name! To better appreciate the significance of God's *non*-response to Moses's question, let's consider what a person's normal response to an inquiry after her name, such as "I am Susie" or "My name is Susie," reveals about a person, beyond the bare revelation of her proper, given name. Most obviously, of course, her response tells us that Susie is a distinct individual. Beyond this, it tells us that Susie is a distinct *female* individual, and beyond even this, that Susie is a distinct female *human* individual. In other words, simply by telling us that her name is Susie, this person implicitly reveals not only that she is a distinct individual, and hence, that she is distinguishable from other distinct individuals, but also that she is identifiable as a member of the class or category of "female human being," and that, as such, this identification serves to distinguish her class from other classes or categories of beings, say, the class of "male human being."

The point, then, is that to tell who you are, to name or identify yourself, is *eo ipso* to categorize yourself, and thus, to distinguish yourself from other categories of individuals. At the same time, to so categorize and distinguish yourself by dint of uttering your proper name is necessarily to limit yourself, that is, to define yourself by and confine yourself to *this* class of individuals as opposed to *that* class of individuals. Accordingly, when God, in response to Moses's inquiry after His identity, simply refers to Himself as "I Am," and not as "I am *So and So*," God effectively reveals that He is beyond all definitional distinctions and categorizing limitations. Put more precisely, by refusing to identify Himself in the usual manner, by refusing, that is, to categorize and define Himself, God indirectly reveals (1) that He shares his Nature with no one, and thus (2) that His Nature is absolutely and supremely unique, and thus (3) that He is utterly beyond all delimiting distinctions and classifications, and thus (4) that He is by nature an *Infinite* Being. In short, by referring to Himself as "I Am," and leaving it at that, the God of the Old Testament obliquely serves notice that He is a fundamentally "formless" Reality!

St. Thomas Aquinas: God as "Altogether Simple"

As a final prominent representative of the God-as-formless school of thought, let's refer to the views of perhaps the foremost Christian philosopher-theologian, Saint Thomas Aquinas (1225–1274). Aquinas, in one of his celebrated works, the *Summa Theologiae*, after presenting his famed five arguments for God's existence (in Volume 1, Question 2), proceeds to delineate God's attributes or properties, beginning in Question 3 with God's "simplicity." By "simplicity" herein Aquinas means to say that God lacks any and all composition or parts, and so, that God is not possessed of a body or any quantitative dimensions, is not reducible to some mode of essential, generic or specific classification, and is not subject to any definitional distinctions or categorical limitations. God, in brief, states Aquinas, is "altogether simple," which is only to say that God is an altogether formless Reality.[4]

Lao Tzu and Thomas Aquinas on God's Formlessness/Simplicity as Basis of God's Other Attributes

Aquinas, therefore, in agreement with the vast majority of the world's great creation myths, as well as the Old Testament's Exodus 3 representation of God, is thus fully in accord with Lao Tzu's declaration in Poem 25 that the "Tao is formless." But recall that Lao Tzu couples the Tao's formlessness with the Tao's perfection, when he writes that "There was something formless *and perfect*..." (Emphasis mine) In so doing, Lao Tzu clearly implies that formlessness and perfection are intrinsically and necessarily linked in the Tao. As it happens, Aquinas, too, after arguing for simplicity (formlessness) as God's first and most fundamental attribute in Question 3, goes on to deduce God's absolute perfection in Question 4. What gives these two men, so disparate in time, temperament, and culture, the right, so to speak, to infer from the Source's formlessness Its absolute perfection? The answer, already alluded in the foregoing paragraphs, is, ironically, the Source's seemingly inscrutable formlessness. For that which is without form or parts transcends all definitional distinctions and categorizing limitations. But that which transcends definitional distinctions and categorizing limitations cannot but be unlimited, flawless, unblemished—in a word, all-perfect. Whence, God is an absolutely perfect Reality.

Moreover, if the Tao is formless and therefore perfect, Lao Tzu further suggests in Poem 25 that It must no less be "Solitary. Unchanging. Infinite. [and] Eternally present." And, once again, Aquinas agrees with this ancient Eastern Sage. For no sooner does Aquinas establish God's simplicity/formlessness and consequent perfection than he proceeds to deduce from these attributes God's infinity (Question 7), unchangeability (Question 9), eternity (Question 10), and unity/solitariness (Question 11), essentially as follows.

That God is infinite follows directly from God's absolute perfection, since that which is absolutely perfect lacks any and all limiting features. But what lacks any and all limiting features is infinite. Whence, God is an infinite Reality. That God is unchangeable no less follows from God's perfection, since that which changes, that which moves, develops or evolves from one state to another state, e.g., from that of an uneducated to that of an educated person, evinces an initial lack of something, in this case, a want of education. But God as sheer perfection lacks nothing. Whence, God is an unchangeable Reality. That God is eternal again follows from God's perfection, as well as from God's infinity and unchangeability, since that which has a temporal beginning or end is subject to change, and thus to imperfection and finitude. Whence, God is an eternal Reality, a Reality totally transcendent of time. Finally, that God is unitary, that is, absolutely unique, follows from all the aforementioned attributes, but most clearly perhaps, from God's root attribute, formlessness or simplicity, since all other things, being defined and categorized by their respective classes, e.g., the class of "human being," are consequently delimited by their shared class membership and, as members of a given class, are distinguishable from those who are not of their class. Now, what is beyond all definitional distinctions and categorical limitations shares Its Nature with no one, but is in fact *sui generis* or absolutely unique. Whence, God is a unitary or absolutely unique Reality.

How Can We Talk about the "Eternal Tao?"

The Reader will doubtless have noticed that the preceding discussion, arguing that it is the Tao's very formlessness that renders any discussion of the Tao ineffable, or ultimately beyond discussion, is replete with discussion about that which is ultimately beyond discussion! For, having determined that the Tao is formless, I went on to show that it is precisely in virtue of the Tao's fundamental formlessness that we can infer the Tao's other attributes, to wit, Its perfection, infinity, unchangeability, eternity, and absolute uniqueness. To be sure, then, I've evidently had a whole lot to say about that which we ultimately can't say anything about.

By way of resolving the riddle of how we can speak about what we can't ultimately speak about, I would first call the Reader's attention to my penchant in the foregoing for such qualifying phrases as, "what can't be *ultimately* spoken about." I've been at pains to write in this modifying manner so as to pave the way for making good on a suggestion I made back in the second paragraph of this chapter, when I wrote that "... to maintain ... that the Tao is ultimately beyond language ... does not thereby entail the conclusion that we can say nothing whatsoever about the Tao, and hence that 'Tao-talk' is utterly meaningless talk." Exactly what, then, are we saying about the Tao when we say that the Tao is formless, perfect, infinite, unchangeable, eternal, and absolutely unique? Which is only to ask: How is it that we can speak meaningfully about that which we can't *ultimately* speak about? And once again, I shall turn to a Westerner, Thomas Aquinas, to help us better understand how it is that, though the Tao be ultimately beyond language, as Lao

Tzu maintains, when we say that the Tao is formless, perfect, and so on, we are yet saying something meaningful about the Tao.

Consider, in the first place, two remarks of Aquinas apropos of our knowledge of God: "Because we cannot know what God is, but rather what He is not, we have no reason for considering how God is, but rather how He is not."[5] And: "True affirmative propositions [statements] can be formed about God."[6] Has Aquinas unwittingly stumbled into a glaring contradiction here, in that he seems to be telling us that we *both can* and *cannot* make affirmative statements about God? My answer is no, Aquinas isn't speaking contradictorily here, and yes, there is a way of reconciling these seemingly irreconcilable Aquinian pronouncements about what we can and cannot say about God. In support thereof, let's examine in some detail what Aquinas had in mind when he uttered these pronouncements, beginning with his assertion that we can only say "what God is not."

To appreciate Aquinas herein, I would first call the Reader's attention to an obvious point, and that is that we can only talk about what we know, and insofar as we know it. Now, as human beings, we know primarily through the medium of concepts. By virtue of conceptualization, we're able to define, categorize, and classify the diversity and multiplicity of our experiences, to look at a number of, say, four-legged, furry, betailed, and (usually) friendly creatures and recognize them all—despite their differences in size, shape, color, temperament, and so on—as members of the class of "dog." As such, conceptualization permits us literally to transcend the confines of space and time, of the here and now, by enabling us to recognize an individual as a member of a given class, such as the class of "dog," irrespective of whether that individual is perceptually present or not, or whether that individual exists in the past, present, or future. In short, we can, via the classificatory function of concepts, appreciate that a dog is a dog, irrespective of time, whether past, present, or future, and irrespective of place, whether perceptually present or not.

Moreover, due to concepts' classificatory/categorizing function, we're able to predicate, to make judgments about members of a class, as when we assert that "Lassie is a dog," or "A maple is a tree." In other words, conceptualization is the basis of propositional language, of our ability to form sentences, to speak and to write, and in general, to communicate *qua* human.

Last but not least, conceptualization is the cognitive foundation of our ability to reason, to infer a conclusion from propositions/judgments standing as evidence for that conclusion, as when we reason, "A maple is a tree, This is a maple, Therefore, this is a tree." In brief, conceptualization, the ability to recognize individuals as members of a given class, is nothing less than the root cause of human communication and thinking, since, save for concepts, we would be unable to form judgments/propositions about members of a class, and so, be unable to speak and to write. And without the ability to form judgments/propositions, we would be unable to draw conclusions from judgments/propositions standing as evidence for said conclusions, and so, be unable to reason. In sum, then, save for concepts, we would be at a loss (1) to classify our experiences, (2) to make judgments about our experiences, and (3) to think about our experiences *qua* human. So much for the good news of human conceptualization.

There is an old adage to the effect that one's strength is but the flip side of one's weakness. And no less does this adage hold true for concepts. As we've noticed, the strength of the concept, the root of specifically human knowing, lies in its classifying and distinguishing function. Indeed, to recognize, say, your pet as a member of the class of "dog," and so, as distinct from other classes of individuals, is no small cognitive feat. Even so, it is the concept's very nobility, its classifying and distinguishing function, that renders it ultimately inadequate as a cognitive link to and representation of the Tao. And this because, as we've abundantly seen, to classify and categorize is per force to delimit, to confine an individual to a given class, and thus to distinguish that individual from individuals belonging to other classes. But the Tao, as we've no less seen, being by nature formless, is *ipso facto* beyond all delimiting classifications and inner distinguishing "parts." And if so, then, when Aquinas writes that we can't know or say what God is, but only what God is not, we see that he has in mind our conceptual mode of knowing. In other words, we can only say what God is not because to think about God conceptually is to reduce that which is beyond all limiting categorization and inner distinguishing parts, namely, the formless God, to our finite conceptual classifications and distinctions. It is to think of the formless God in a way that God is *not*, namely, as possessed of form, and so, effectively to relegate God entirely to the formal status of a creature, of a being existing among and distinct from other beings. It is, in short, to strip God of God's true status as the I Am, as Existence Itself.[7]

Which brings us to Aquinas's other, seemingly contradictory, assertion, namely, that we can make true affirmative statements about God. How might we square this assertion with Aquinas's no less emphatic declaration that we can only say what God is not? I believe the answer lies, in the first place, in noting that, when Aquinas avers that we can only say what God is not, he isn't proposing thereby that our knowledge of God is simply and entirely negative. That is, Aquinas is not telling us what God is not in the same way that someone might assert that a dog is not a cat, not a komodo dragon, not a human being, not a fungus, and so on. Such knowledge, if indeed we can call it that, is *absolutely* negative; it provides us no clue whatsoever as to what a dog actually and intrinsically *is*. Indeed, with such so-called knowledge the process of exclusion could go on forever, and we would be not one wit closer to knowing what a dog truly is!

Now, we've seen that, according to Aquinas, given our conceptual mode of knowing, when we state that God is formless, perfect, and so on, we're actually saying that God has no form, is not imperfect, and like negative characterizations. But, be it noted, in so saying we're not speaking merely exclusively, we're not simply and absolutely saying what God is not, as when we say that a dog is not a human being. And why not? Because in referring to God as formless, etc.—which indeed we must, if God is truly God—we're attributing to God properties that are *necessarily and uniquely God's own*. That is, we're stating, in effect, that God, and God alone, is formless, that God, and God alone, is not imperfect, and so on. Which can only mean one thing: When we state that God is formless, etc., we're actually uttering, as Aquinas maintains, true affirmative statements about what God, and God alone, *is*, notwithstanding our limited conceptual grasp of what God is.

Accordingly, for Aquinas, there is no real contradiction in asserting that we can and cannot affirm statements of God, if we bear in mind the following. Insofar as the formless God necessarily exceeds our conceptual grasp, we can only say what God is not. But insofar as formlessness, perfection, infinity, etc., are properties absolutely unique to God, we are, however inadequately, truly speaking affirmatively about God, truly saying that God alone is formless, perfect, infinite, and all the rest. The upshot of these musings on what we can and cannot say of God, for Aquinas, is that "God-talk" remains meaningful talk, talk in keeping with our human modes of experience and understanding, even if such talk signifies a Reality that will ever exceed human experience and understanding.[8]

Does Lao Tzu Regard "God-Talk" as Meaningful Talk?

Finally, while Aquinas may help us appreciate how "God-talk" is ultimately meaningful talk, does the *Tao Te Ching* provide any reason to think that Lao Tzu concurs with Aquinas in this "God-talking" respect? I submit that, while it is clear that the *Tao Te Ching* offers no such elaborate discussion, as does Aquinas, of how God-talk is ultimately meaningful talk; and, truth to be told, it is highly unlikely that Lao Tzu even expressly bothered his head with any such theological conundrum; even so, when we peruse the pages of the *Tao Te Ching*, we notice that, wittingly or no, Lao Tzu furnishes an implicit, and therefore *in-need-of-being-developed*, reason for holding that he views God-talk as ultimately meaningful talk. In which regard, consider the following excerpt from Poem 21:

> Since before time and space were,
> the Tao is.
> It is beyond *is* and *is not*.

In this terse but fertile excerpt, Lao Tzu echoes the Old Testament and Aquinas's non-categorical/non-definitional, and hence, *sui generis* view of the Source. As Lao Tzu notes, the Tao simply *is*, or, if you prefer, and in agreement with the Old Testament, the Tao can only be signified as the "I Am," or, in the vein of Aquinas, as "Existence Itself." For this reason, "the Tao is beyond *is* [So and So]," that is, beyond our conceptual affirmations, beyond our limited and limiting classifications and definitions. In this sense, Lao Tzu effectively says, when we attempt to affirm what the Tao that utterly transcends all delimiting conceptualizations is, such affirmations, being the product of delimiting conceptualization, tell us not what the Tao that simply is *is*, but rather what the Tao that simply is *is not*.

But no less, writes Lao Tzu, is "the Tao beyond *is not* [So and So]," beyond our conceptual negations. This means not only that the Tao can't be fathomed by sheer negation alone, by simply saying what the Tao is not, even unto infinity, as was noted above, but, much more importantly, that the Tao by virtue of the fact that It simply *is*, and so, transcends all categorical and definitional delimitations, is an absolutely Unique Reality. Now, to affirm that the Tao is absolutely Unique, and so transcends all categorizing and defining forms, entails, as was noted, the further affirmation that the Tao is formless, perfect, infinite, and so on. But beyond this, it entails, as was also noted, the affirmation that the Tao, and the Tao alone, is formless, perfect, infinite, and so on. In other words, the Tao, so to speak, negates the negations. For, though our conceptual mode of knowing necessarily limits the Tao, and insofar, reveals what the Tao is *not*, this doesn't mean that our assertions about the Tao are merely assertions about what the Tao is not. Rather, insofar as our assertions about the Tao ascribe to the Tao attributes that are absolutely unique to the Tao, our assertions constitute true affirmations about the Tao, even though, given our conceptual mode of knowing, we can't fully grasp the significance of these affirmations.

It would seem, then, that there exists no great philosophical breach between Aquinas and Lao Tzu on God-talk as meaningful talk. Lao Tzu implicitly agrees with Aquinas's contention that, given God/the Tao's uniqueness (formless Nature), God/the Tao exceeds our affirmations, while yet maintaining that, precisely because of God/the Tao's uniqueness, our affirmations do express what God/the Tao is, albeit in a less than comprehensive manner. Hence, for Lao Tzu, no less than for Aquinas, God-talk must be accounted meaningful talk, talk that does no violence to human understanding, notwithstanding that such talk signifies a Reality that will ever exceed human understanding.[9]

Grasping the Tao Intuitively: Preliminary Remarks

So much for how we can meaningfully talk about and know certain of the "eternal Tao's" primary attributes. However, before proceeding to the next chapter, it should be noted that, for Lao Tzu, the conceptual mode of knowing the Tao must be transcended in favor of a far higher and more perfect way of knowing the Tao. That we must transcend our normal conceptual mode of knowing, if we would more fully know the Tao, Lao Tzu hints at when he writes:

> The Tao is ungraspable.
> How can her mind be at one with it?
> Because she doesn't cling to ideas. (Poem 21)[10]

But if it is not by ideas alone, by normal conceptual knowing, that we are "at one with the Tao," then by what presumably more perfect means of knowing do we realize this oneness? Lao Tzu's answer he expresses variously throughout the *Tao Te Ching*. Thus, he writes:

> The Master observes the world
> but trusts his inner vision. (Poem 12)

> Approach it [the Tao] and there is no beginning;
> follow it and there is no end.
> You can't know it, but you can be it... (Poem 14)

> When the body's intelligence declines,
> cleverness and knowledge step forth. (Poem 18):

> Without looking out your window,
> you can see the essence of the Tao. (Poem 47)

And finally,

> Your intellect will never grasp [my teachings]...
> How can you grasp their meaning?...
> [L]ook inside your heart. (Poem 70)

What Lao Tzu alludes to in the foregoing citations is an ability cultivated by all creative types, including most especially, *spiritually* creative types, namely, the cultivation of one's intuitive faculty.[11] Here, in advocating the nurturing of intuition as the paramount cognitive vehicle to union with the Tao, Lao Tzu is in complete accord with virtually all spiritual sages, past and present. For whereas conceptual knowing discerns a person, place, thing, or event by categorizing it and thus by regarding it as separate from other persons, places, things, and events, intuitive knowing apprehends a person, place, thing, or event through a direct and immediate experience of, and insight ("inner vision") into, the essence of that person, place, thing, and event—all of which Lao Tzu doubtless means to convey when he declares, "You can't know [the Tao], but you can *be* [that is, directly experience] it..." At the same time, intuition, which is typically signaled by some sort of physiological response, is for that reason often described in terms of such bodily based metaphors as "heart knowledge," "body knowledge," and even "gut knowledge"—which again, Lao Tzu doubtless intends when he speaks of the "body's intelligence" and exhorts each of us to "look inside your heart."

Having but briefly introduced Lao Tzu's view that conceptual knowing must be superseded in favor of intuitive knowing, if we are ever to realize our connection to the Tao, and having preliminarily indicated the nature of intuitive knowing, we must for the time being leave the matter at that, until we can better appreciate both the nature and function of intuition, as well as Lao Tzu's in many ways unique proposal for realizing this intuitive, and therefore, unified state of consciousness. To this end, let us begin from the beginning with a look in Chapter 2 at another of the Tao's attributes, the Tao as Creator, and consider what main consequences the Tao's creative activity holds for creation, in general, and human creation, in particular.

Notes

1. If for some unfathomable reason you bypassed the Introduction, please be advised that hereinafter all references in this book to the *Tao Te Ching* are from the Stephen Mitchell translation thereof, 2nd Edition (NY: Perennial Classics, 2000).

2. The Tao's fundamental formlessness Lao Tzu also means to suggest when he refers to the Tao as "... the eternal void: filled with infinite possibilities." *Tao Te Ching*, Poem 4. See too in this "void"-respect *Ibid.*, Poems 5, 6, 28. Then again, Lao Tzu alludes to the Tao's formlessness when he declares: "All things are born of being. Being is born of non-being [or of that which is beyond being, form, and categorization]." *Ibid.*, Poem 40.

3. For a good, easily accessible compilation of myths in general and creation myths in particular, see J.F. Berlein, *Parallel Myths* (New York: Ballantine Books, 1994). In line with this ancient view that the cosmos is begotten of "Chaos" or the "Abyss," Lao Tzu writes: "The world is formed from the void..." (Poem 28)

4. See Thomas Aquinas, *Summa Theologiae, Volume 1: The Existence of God*, Part One, Question 3. Thomas Gilby, O.P., editor { New York: Image Books, 1969). Interestingly, the idea of the Source's fundamental formlessness is also found in the other great Western religions. Thus, ancient Jewish Cabalism speaks of *En Soph*, the Reality beyond even Jahweh, and ancient Islamic Suffism refers to *Al Haqq*, the Reality beyond Allah Itself. The same idea is likewise found among the so-called Pagans. For example, it is alluded to by the pre-Socratic philosophers Anaximander (ca. 610–547 BCE) in his doctrine of "the Indeterminate" and Parmenides (ca. 515–450 BCE) in his doctrine of "the One," and expressly espoused by Plato (428–348 BCE) in his notion of "the Good," the Reality beyond the Forms.

5. *Ibid.*, Question 3, Preface. In fact, states Aquinas, "This is the ultimate human knowledge of God: to know that one does not know God." (Italics mine) My translation of "Hoc illud est ultimum cognitionis humanae de Deo: quod sciat se Deum nescire." St. Thomas Aquinas, *Questiones Disputatae*, Vol. 1: *De Potentia Dei*, Question 7, Article 5, Response to the fourteenth objection. (Domus Editorialis Marietti: Romae, 1942).

6. See *Ibid.*, Question 13, Article 12.

7. See *Ibid.*, Question 3, Article 4. Also see *Ibid.*, Question 13, Article 11.

8. This is my rendering of *Ibid.*, Question12, Article 12, Reply and Question 13, Articles 1–12.

9. Chapter 2, wherein I discuss the Tao as Creator, provides a further reason why "God-talk," though ultimately beyond comprehension, is yet meaningful talk.

10. Also see in this idea-transcending regard, *Tao Te Ching*, Poems 1, 12, 14, 16, 47, 59, 64, 70 and 71.

11. Lao Tzu expresses similar views in *Ibid.*, Poems 27, 50, 54, and 67.

CHAPTER TWO

The Tao as Creator

> The Tao is called the Great Mother:
> empty yet inexhaustible, it gives birth
> to infinite worlds.
>
> *Lao Tzu, Tao Te Ching, Poem 6*

The Tao as Creator

Poem 51 of the Tao Te Ching begins with the remark:

> Every being in the universe is an expression of the Tao.

Here, Lao Tzu evidently speaks of the Tao as the supreme creative force. But precisely how are we to understand the Tao's creative activity? Is creation, in keeping with Western philosophic and religious tradition, an act whereby the Source creates "*ex nihilo*"? That is, does the Tao create "out of nothing" save Its Own infinite nature and power, a finite, eternally dependent creation, thereby establishing the infinite Tao's absolute distinction from and transcendence of Its creation? The answer is an emphatic no, and in support thereof consider another creation-passage from Poem 34:

> The great Tao flows everywhere.
> All things are born from it,
> yet it doesn't create them.
> It pours itself into its work…

I would call the Reader's attention especially to two phrases in this passage: "... it doesn't create them" and "It pours itself into its work ..." In stating that the Tao "doesn't create" beings, Lao Tzu implies that beings, though "born" of the Tao, are not brought into existence "*ex nihilo*." In stating that the Tao "pours itself into its work," Lao Tzu indicates the way in which beings are "born" of the Tao, namely, by an act of divine Self-expression, an eternal "pouring forth" of the infinite Tao's Own substance into Its (on this plane) 3-D forms. In other words, for Lao Tzu, and indeed, for most Eastern philosophers and theologians, there exists no radical distinction between Creator and created. As opposed to the common Western view of creation, the common Eastern view holds that the infinite Source, being all there is and all there ever will be, can only create of Itself, of Its Own infinite substance, and thus that all creatures, great and small, are fundamentally and essentially divine expressions of the Source.

The Tao: Transcendent *and* Immanent

Now, to affirm that the Tao creates by "pouring itself" into Its creation is not to imply that the Tao "loses Itself" in Its creation, that the Tao is totally confined to and contained within Its creation, after the manner of water being poured into a vessel. The Tao, as we've seen, is an infinite, an absolutely unlimited Reality. As such, the Tao will ever be transcendent of Its creation, and can in no wise be reduced to or defined solely in terms of Its creation. But neither does this mean that the Tao has absolutely no connection or association with Its creation. As an infinite Reality, the Tao must be "everywhere," and hence must be at once ever transcendent of *and* immanent or inherently present in Its creation! Nor does the *Tao Te Ching* merely imply as much when it affirms the Tao's infinity (see Poem 25). That the Tao is an immanent Reality the *Tao Te Ching* specifically alludes to in such passages as:

> [The Tao} is always present within you (Poem 6)

and

> [The Tao] is merged with all things . . . (Poem 34)

That the Tao is a transcendent Reality, the *Tao Te Ching* metaphorically indicates when it states:

> [The Tao's] net covers the whole universe.
> And though its meshes are wide,
> it doesn't let a thing slip through. (Poem 73)

And finally, that the Tao is at once an immanent *and* transcendent Reality the *Tao Te Ching* again metaphorically intimates when it declares:

> [The Tao] flows through all things,
> inside and outside . . . (Poem 25)

Thus, and as Lao Tzu sees it, as an infinite Reality, the Tao cannot but be both transcendent of and immanent in Its creation. For, were the Tao purely immanent in Its creation, It would be reduced to and limited by Its creation, thereby divesting the Tao of Its infinite status by relegating It to that of a sort of super, but still fundamentally, finite being. On the other hand, were the Tao totally transcendent of Its creation, this would mean that there is some place, specifically Its creation, where the Tao doesn't exist, thereby likewise stripping the Tao of Its infinite, Its boundless, status by denying Its ubiquity, its "everywhereness." The technical term for the former, radically immanent view of the Tao is *pantheism*, the view that the Tao is no more and no less than Its creation. The technical term for the latter, radically transcendent view of the Tao is *deism*, the view that the Tao, after begetting creation, exists in utter, eternal, and even uncaring separation from Its creaturely progeny. Against both a pantheistic and a deistic rendering of the Tao's creative activity the *Tao Te Ching* holds that the infinite Tao, precisely because It is infinite, is at one and the same time transcendent of and immanent in Its creation, a view that nowadays is typically styled *panentheism*, which is to say the view that "All is in God even as God is in all."[1]

Panentheism: A Profound Mystery

Clearly, in maintaining that the Tao is at one and the same time transcendent of and immanent in Its creation, we encounter a profound mystery, and therefore a view that will ever exceed our human comprehension. Still, if we can never hope to fathom the length, breadth, and depth of such a view, this isn't to say that it is a meaningless view, that it is totally and hopelessly beyond human understanding and experience. For one thing, we can at least understand that, *if* the Tao is verily an infinite Reality, then it stands well to reason that, *qua* Creator, the Tao must be both transcendent of and immanent in Its creation. Either this, or the Tao is reduced to a finite, and so, a *non*-boundless, reality—in short, to a reality other than the Tao! Otherwise put, we can at least understand *that* the Tao must be both transcendent of and immanent in Its creation, even if we can't fully comprehend or appreciate *how* It manages this simultaneous feat!

Then again, historically, when attempting to make some sense of a mystery, a common literary device has been to resort to metaphor (a figure of speech in which a word or phrase that usually designates one thing is used to designate another) in an effort to approximate, to furnish some semblance of, an explanation. In which explanatory regard, a favored way to illustrate how the Tao can be at once immanent and transcendent in relation to creation is to liken It figuratively to the sun and its irradiations. For, just as the sun retains its identity and integrity even as it emits its rays, and hence, doesn't "lose itself" in its fiery emanations, so the infinite Tao retains Its transcendent identity and integrity even as It "pours Itself" into Its creation, without thereby "losing Itself" in Its creaturely emanations or Self-manifestations.

Panentheism: East and West

Should panentheism still seem a rather large theological pill to swallow, Iwould simply note that the overall idea of the Source being at once transcendent of and immanent in Its creation is no less proclaimed by orthodox Jewish, Christian, and Islamic religious traditions, even if in somewhat muted fashion. Nevertheless, if overall it is true to say that East meets West on this theological score, there remains a vast difference between the Eastern and Western interpretation of this theological principle. The East, as we saw, regards creation as an act of divine Self-manifestation, a "pouring forth" of the Source's Own infinite substance into Its creaturely forms. As such, the infinite Source, while remaining ever transcendent of Its creation, is at the same time immanently present *as* Its creation. In other words, for the East, creatures, in virtue of the Source's immanence, *are* the Source expressing Itself in and through Its multitudinous and diverse creaturely forms. The West, on the other hand, and as we likewise saw, views the Source as creating "*ex nihilo*," thereby establishing a radical and unbridgeable distinction between the Infinite Source and Its doubtless large, perhaps even infinitely extended, but still eternally finite creation. For this reason, the infinite Source, while remaining ever transcendent of Its creation, is also said to be immanent, not *as*, but *in* Its creation.

In other words, for the West, the Source's immanence *in* creation doesn't entail the Eastern view that creatures *are* the Source expressing Itself in and through Its multitudinous and diverse creaturely forms. For the West, the Source is rather *in* creation as the eternally sustaining and all-powerful *Cause of the existence* of Its multitudinous and diverse creaturely forms. In sum, we might articulate the differing Eastern-Western viewpoints on the Source's immanence as follows: whereas, for the East, creatures are of the selfsame substance as the Source, for the West, creatures *have* the Source immanently within them as the supreme and ever-sustaining Cause of their existence.[2]

Our Nature's Natural, Tao-Given Lovingness

We've seen that, for the *Tao Te Ching*, creation *is* the Tao Self-expressing Itself in and through Its manifold creaturely forms, which is only to say that creatures are one and all *divine* manifestations of the infinite Tao. Now, the implications of this Taoist view for the inherent dignity of all beings, "great and small," could not be plainer. So I won't elaborate on the obvious. I would, however, again call the Reader's attention to Poem 51, and this time to the second stanza, wherein Lao Tzu implicitly reveals what is doubtless the principal way in which creatures—and here, let us simplify matters by singling out *human* creatures—manifest the Tao's divinity.

In this remarkable stanza, after once again proclaiming the Tao's creative activity—"The Tao gives birth to all beings"—Lao Tzu forthwith proceeds to delineate how the Tao relates to Its Self-creations. The Tao, he writes,

> nourishes them, maintains them,
> cares for them, comforts them, protects them,
> takes them back to itself,
> creating without possessing,
> acting without expecting,
> guiding without interfering.

That is, like a loving "mother"—a favorite image of Lao Tzu when speaking of the Tao's creative activity (see Poems 6 and 25)—not only does the Tao nourish, maintain, care for, comfort, and protect her children. Beyond even these noble expressions of loving concern, the Tao is nonpossessive of Her children, doesn't expect anything in return from Her children, and doesn't interfere in Her children's lives. In short, if nonpossessiveness, nonattachment, and noninterference are unmistakable signs of unconditional love, then the Tao's love is beyond that of a loving mother; the Tao is nothing less than a *perfectly* loving mother, a mother who loves Her children selflessly and unreservedly.

Nor is this all, states the *Tao Te Ching*. Indeed, the Tao's love for Her children exceeds even that of a perfectly loving mother! To appreciate this statement, I refer the Reader to the previous chapter. There, as you recall, on the way to discussing how we can talk about the "eternal Tao," we noticed that the Tao's primary attribute is Its "formlessness," and that in virtue of this attribute, we may infer that the Tao is "perfect," "unchanging," "infinite," "eternally present," and "solitary" (see Poem 25). We also noticed that to speak of the

Tao as formless means that, in Itself, the Tao is "without parts," and more precisely, totally beyond any and all limiting classifications and definitional distinctions. Which conclusions beget, in their turn, yet another mystery-laden conclusion about the Tao. And that is that, if the Tao possesses no distinguishing and classifying parts, then the Tao must be *identical to,* not distinct from, Its attributes. To suggest otherwise, to suggest that the Tao is distinct from Its attributes, is effectively to maintain that the Tao merely *shares in* or *has* an attribute, as when we say, "Susie is brilliant," and mean thereby, not that Susie is herself the class of brilliant!, but only and more modestly that Susie is a *member of,* and thus shares in, the class of brilliant. Thus, if the Tao, *à la* a person, place, or thing, in a word, a creature, merely shares in a given class of attribute, then the Tao is both distinct from and limited by and to that class of attribute, and insofar, is not a formless Reality. But if not a formless Reality, then of course neither is the Tao a perfect, infinite, eternal, unchanging, or solitary (totally unique) Reality. Whence, the mysterious and inescapable conclusion that the *Tao is and can only be identical to what we say about It.*

Having shown how and why the Tao *is* Its attributes, we're now better placed to appreciate in what sense the Tao's love for Her children may be said to exceed even that of a perfectly loving mother. And that would be as follows: If the Tao is the selfsame as Its attributes, to affirm that the Tao is perfectly loving is actually and more properly to affirm that the Tao is Perfect, Infinite, Unchanging, and Eternal Love Itself. But if this is true, then we may draw a further and no less remarkable conclusion: namely, that if creatures—and, once again, let's stick for present purposes to *human* creatures—are of the selfsame substance as the Tao, which is to say, are the Tao expressing Itself in and through Its created forms, then, from the perspective of the *Tao Te Ching,* our True Nature must be naturally loving! All of which we might epitomize inferentially as follows: The Tao is Love. Our True Nature is an expression of the Tao. Accordingly, our True Nature is by nature loving.

Our True Nature Is Naturally Loving?

Almost certainly, a naturally loving view of our True Nature will strike even the most liberally minded among us as unduly sanguine. And they could certainly make a strong case to the contrary. For one thing, they might point out that such a view is highly uncongenial to one's personal experience, in particular, and historical experience, in general. For another, they might flatly contend that such a view flies in the face of sheer common sense. For yet another, especially if they're of the Christian persuasion, they might be inclined to disagree with said view on the grounds that it runs counter to the doctrine of "Original Sin." Then again, if they're of a scholarly bent, they might see fit to note that such an estimate of our nature has been roundly rejected by virtually every thinker, past and present, who has ever pondered the nature of human nature. Last but by no means least, they might direct our attention to the fact that the existence of laws, morality, and religion in, as far as we can determine, all cultures, past and present, plainly suggests that we humans are congenitally in need of legal guidelines, moral standards, and religious sanctions, if not to control and manage us, then at the very least to rein in our often less than loving impulses and actions. In the face of such formidable objections, even were one to grant that, given his assumptions, Lao Tzu's naturally loving assessment of our True Nature makes logical sense, one might still want to question whether his assessment herein makes any real evidential sense, whether, that is, his estimate of our True Nature is at all in keeping with the way things really and truly are.

The Problem: We've "Forgotten" our "True Nature"

That the *Tao Te Ching* offers no express response to the foregoing objections to the naturally loving status of our True Nature will be evident to anyone who has perused this spiritual classic. But clearly, a man of Lao Tzu's savvy and caliber could hardly have failed to notice the apparent contradiction between a naturally loving view of our True Nature and the fact that we humans sometimes act in less than loving ways. Nor is this simply a matter of historical conjecture, since

Lao Tzu supplies what amounts to an *implicit* answer to the aforementioned apparent contradiction. And that is that the reason we humans sometimes act in other than loving ways is that we've "lost" sight of (Poem 38), have "forgotten" (Poem 18), who we truly are, namely, loving expressions of the Tao That is Love Itself. Such "forgetfulness" has begotten the illusory belief that our "true nature" (Poem 65)[3] is separate from the Tao. Which illusory "separatist" belief has led in its turn to the further and no less illusory belief that we lack the power, the natural capacity, to act in a consistently loving way.

Such is Lao Tzu's essential, albeit implicit, answer to why, though our True Nature be naturally loving, we still sometimes acquit ourselves in other than loving ways. But before we can better appreciate his answer, we'll first need to examine in some detail the "event" that precipitated our "forgetfulness" of our "True Nature" and consequent belief in our *non*naturally loving condition. This "event," in keeping with Western theological parlance, I shall designate the Tao's "Fall," and concerning which I shall devote Chapter 3.

Notes

1. That Aquinas agrees with a panentheistic view of God's creative activity is evident from the following:"Multiplicity can proceed from unity in three ways... Thirdly, by effusion, as when many rivers rise from one source, and water from a spring spills into many streams. In this last comparison there is some likeness to the going out and distribution of distinct goods from the divine goodness, *though here no lessening of the original is involved in the separation and multiplication, for the divine goodness remains undivided in its essence, unspent, and simple*." (Emphasis mine) From *Exposition on the Divine Names*, Part 2, Lecture 6. Cited in *Saint Thomas Aquinas: Philosophical Texts*, trans., Thomas Gilby (NY: Oxford University Press, 1960), p. 130. See also St. Thomas Aquinas, *Summa Theologica* ,Volume One, Question 44, Article 1 (NY: Benziger Brothers, Inc., 1946).

2. A point Aquinas argues in his *Summa Theologica*, Volume One, Question 8 (NY: Benzinger Brothers, Inc., 1946). I would just remark that, in my opinion, how we differ from God is a mystery second only to that of God Itself. I also maintain that the common Eastern view of God's immanence is more consistent than the common Western view, and that Western theologians and philosophers of religion are far from successful in their

efforts to justify God's immanence in creation, while yet safeguarding God's infinite distinction therefrom.

3. Other designations for our "True Nature" that Lao Tzu employs in the *Tao Te Ching* are "primal self" (Poem 28) and "primal identity" (Poem 56).

CHAPTER THREE

The Tao's "Fall"

The great Tao flows everywhere.
All things are born from it . . .

Lao Tzu, Tao Te Ching, Poem 34

The Tao's Willful "Fall"

In Chapter 2, we examined what is doubtless the most remarkable consequence of the Tao's creative activity: that each and every creature, as an immanent expression of the Tao's infinite Nature, is, by nature, divine. A principal corollary to this consequence, we further noticed, is that, as the Tao is Love, and we are expressions of the Tao, then, appearances notwithstanding!, our True Nature is naturally loving. This consequence and principal corollary thereof we may take to be the main upside of the Tao's creative activity.

But there is also a quasi-downside to the Tao's decision to create that is inherent in the act of creation itself. This inherent "downside" we may characterize as the Tao's *willing descent into dualism*. By this characterization I allude to the Tao's voluntary decision to manifest Itself, via creation, as Its many and diverse forms. The price of this decision to express Itself immanently as Its manifold forms was twofold. First, the Tao had to choose to "forget" Its undifferentiated oneness or formlessness so as to regard Itself as possessed of distinct forms. Second, and as a direct result of the Tao's willful forgetting of Its formlessness, the Tao had to accept "dualism," the illusory belief in Its expressed forms' separation, not only from one another, but even, and especially as regards Its *human* forms, from the Tao Itself. In other words, if creation betokens, as we've seen, a cosmos, and thus a multiplicity and variety of unified forms, then only in forgetting Its formlessness and allowing Itself to view "reality" as composed of distinct and varied forms existing in separation from one another, could creation—the Tao expressing Itself in and through Its manifold forms— occur.

What I've labeled the Tao's "willing descent into dualism" may be viewed as Lao Tzu's rendering of the Eastern version of the Western "Fall" motif. But unlike the Western version, which takes place in time and space (the Garden of Eden), involves human fault (Adam and Eve's free decision to disobey Yahweh and eat of the "Tree of the Knowledge of Good and Evil"), and entails, as punishment, humans' separation from God, and thus physical, psychological, and relational suffering (Original Sin), the Tao's descent into dualism takes place outside of time and space (from eternity), involves no fault, human or divine, and is the result of the Tao's free decision to Self-express Itself in and through Its manifold forms.[1]

Lao Tzu's Depictions of the Tao's "Fall"

Lao Tzu alludes to the "Fall" motif in several passages of the *Tao Te Ching*. For instance, in Poem 42, he writes:

> The Tao gives birth to One.
> One gives birth to Two.
> Two gives birth to Three.
> Three gives birth to all things.

In language that is as Spartan as it is profound, Lao Tzu tells us that the "eternal Tao" first prepares for Its descent into the dualistic realm of space and time by "giving birth to One," or what we may more precisely, even if less elegantly, style, 'The Primal Concept *One*.' More to the point, the Tao that is utterly beyond form, and thus beyond the dualistic constraints of space and time, elects, as preliminary to Its descent into dualism, to conceive of a 'Primal Conceptual Design' that would serve as a 'Primal Prototype' or 'Blueprint' for Its manifold Self-expressions.

This 'Primal Conceptual Design' Lao Tzu indirectly refers to when next he writes: "One gives birth to Two." That is, the 'Design' in question is "Two," namely, the 'Primal Composition.' But why the 'Primal Composition'? The answer is that conceptual knowing, as we abundantly observed in Chapter 1, necessarily entails distinct yet related parts, or, more simply, 'composition'—whether through the distinguishing of classes, as when we distinguish the class of human from that of reptile, or through distinguishing the components that essentially constitute a class, as when we define "human" as "animal with reason."

Now, the 'Primal Composition' that serves as 'Primal conceptual Design' or 'Pattern' for the Tao's creative Self-expressions Taoism traditionally designates "Yin" and "Yang." Generally speaking, and for present purposes, Yin may be viewed as the primal "feminine" constitutive co-principle and model of *all* creation, Yang, as the primal "masculine" constitutive co-principle and model of all creation.[2] Yin and Yang, in short, are the formless Tao's, as it were, 'first conceptual move,' Its first, overriding, and all-encompassing conceptual 'Design' for Its manifold of created Self-expressions.

The Tao's 'Primal Yin/Yang Conceptual Design' for creation means that not only are all the forms in which the Tao chooses to Self-manifest and Self-reflect Itself effectively "male" or "female"; even more significantly, it means that though males, human or otherwise, typically embody more of Yang energy, and females, human or otherwise, typically manifest more of Yin energy, males and females, as expressions of the Tao's primal creative 'Design,' are nevertheless fundamentally and complementarily "composed" of both Yin and Yang principles. As Daniel Reid explains:

> Contrary to common misconceptions, yin and yang are not two different types of energy, but rather two complementary poles of the same basic energy, like the positive and negative poles of an electric current

> or amagnetic field. Yin and yang are reciprocal states of cyclic change, polarphases of the rhythmic transformations of energy.[3]

The view that all created forms, be they male or female, manifest and reflect the Tao's 'Primal' Yin/Yang Conceptual Design,' Lao Tzu figuratively indicates thusly:

> All things have their backs to the female [Yin]
> and stand facing the male [Yang]. (Poem 42)

Moreover, given each created form's fundamentally composite Yin/Yang nature, the overall task in life, the way in which we will finally come to realize wholeness, happiness, and liberation by dint of consciously reuniting with the Tao, becomes one of learning to strike the delicate balance between these Yin and Yang "sides" of our nature—a point Lao Tzu clearly has in mind when he declares:

> When male [Yang] and female [Yin] combine,
> all things achieve harmony. (Poem 42)*

But a 'Design,' even a 'Primal Design,' is one thing, applying and realizing that 'Design,' another thing entirely. For this to happen, for the Tao's 'Primal Yin/Yang Conceptual Design' to express Itself in the world of forms, the Tao must "descend" into the illusory world of dualism. But how else can the Tao do this, save by regarding Its primal Yin co-principle and model of creation as "separate" from Its complementary primal Yang co-principle and model of creation? Only in this way can creation happen. Only in this way can the Tao commence Its "descent into dualism," take on form, and thereby express Itself, first, through Its primally "masculine" and "feminine" Self-expressions, and then through the "creative interactions," if you will, of Its primally

---

*How we go about reconnecting with the Tao will be the topic of Chapters 6, 7, and 8.

"feminine" and "masculine" Self-expressions. In other words, through the creative 'commingling' of Its Yin and Yang co-principles, the Tao's 'Grand Design' is realized, as creation, the cosmos, dualism, space and time, the realm of forms, the Tao's manifold of Self-manifestations, call it what you will, is born. All of which creative Self-expressing by and of the Tao Lao Tzu epitomizes in typically understated fashion: "Two gives birth to Three."

Finally, having begotten "Three," having given birth to creation, to the world of Self-expressed forms, patterned as they are on the Tao's 'Primal Yin/Yang Conceptual Design', the Tao is now free to create in the 'natural' way, which is to say, through the "creative interactions" of Its variegated Yin/Yang Self-expressions, as "Three gives birth to all things." And with this last creative move, the Tao's "descent into dualism," Its willful "Fall," is complete.

Now, if an economy of expression characterizes Lao Tzu's depiction of the Tao's "Fall" in Poem 42, in Poem 51 he furnishes another, somewhat more elaborate, depiction of the "Fall" motif, when he states:

> Every being in the universe
> is an expression of the Tao.
> It springs into existence,
> unconscious, perfect, free,
> takes on a physical body,
> lets circumstances complete it.

In this extraordinary, slightly less laconic, passage, Lao Tzu makes three principal points. The first point is that all beings are "expressions of the Tao." The second point speaks to our *initial* mode of existence as expressions of the Tao, namely, as "unconscious, perfect, free." And the third point alludes to our descent into dualism, our "Fall" from our original mode of existence: "Every being . . . takes on a physical body, lets circumstances complete it." The nature and significance of point one I've amply discussed in Chapter 2. The nature and significance of point two warrants a word of explanation. And in this chapter, while I've examined point three to the extent of indicating the twofold price the Tao had to pay for Its "Fall" (Its "forgetfulness" of Its inherent formlessness and Its acceptance of the illusion of dualism), it would behoove us to consider with respect to this third point two corollary questions: *What does it mean to affirm that the Tao "forgets" Its undifferentiated oneness?* and, granting the Tao's forgetfulness herein, *Why would the Tao elect to create in the first place?* Before proceeding to investigate these further questions posed by point three, let's first take up point two, and consider what Lao Tzu intends when he proclaims our original mode of existence to be "unconscious, perfect, free."

In asserting that our inceptive mode of existence as expressions of the Tao is "unconscious, perfect, free," Lao Tzu alludes to a mythic motif variously referred to as the "Golden Age,"[4] the "Dreamtime" or "Dreamlike Age,"[5] or as is customary in the West, the "Garden of Eden" or "Edenic Age."[6] Yet, however we designate this motif, its fundamental, shared idea is that, "in the beginning," and prior to the "Fall," all beings existed in a state of perfection and freedom, marked, most notably, by a condition of union, harmony, bliss, and peace between creature and Creator, and between creatures themselves.

But if this suffices to explain Lao Tzu's depiction of the "Golden-Age" state as "perfect" and "free," what are we to make of his additional reference to this state as "unconscious"? By "unconscious" herein does he mean to imply that this primal, unified state is one in which beings were completely bereft of consciousness or awareness, as when we say of a boxer that the poor fellow was "knocked unconscious"?! That Lao Tzu can't have this popular understanding of "unconscious" in mind becomes apparent when we recall that he likewise designates this Edenic state as "free." For, if in that perfect state beings were verily "free," this plainly presupposes some degree of awareness on their part as a minimal condition of choice, since anyone "unconscious" in the popular sense of the term can hardly be said to be aware, and thus to possess even this bottom-line condition of choice.

If, then, it is a good bet that in this passage Lao Tzu doesn't mean "unconscious" in its commonplace sense, in what sense can he be using this term? I submit that his use of "unconscious" in this context is meant to convey an original *non-dualistic* state of being. To make sense of this, I would, in the first place, make note of the contemporary psychological view that the unconscious is a *non-discriminatory* faculty. That is, the unconscious, say today's psychologists, simply takes in and absorbs whatever we do, say, feel, and think, good, bad, or indifferent (1) without bothering to distinguish between good, bad, and indifferent, and (2) without bothering to assess whether we're even serious about or aware of what we do say, feel, and think, good, bad, or indifferent. As such, the "unconscious" becomes an apt, albeit terse, metaphor for an original non-dualistic state of existence, the aforementioned "Golden-Age" state wherein beings were harmoniously at one with the Tao, prior to the Tao's decision to descend and commence Its career in the realm of (seemingly) distinct and variegated created forms. Which "descent" and "career" Lao Tzu simply renders: "Every ... expression of the Tao ... takes on a physical body, lets circumstances complete it."

N.B.: The Tao Isn't a *Complete* Amnesiac!

Having examined why Lao Tzu speaks of our pre-Fallen condition as "unconscious, perfect, free," let's now ask and attempt to resolve the two corollary questions that arise in consequence of the Tao's free decision to Self-express Itself in creation by "taking on a physical body." In this section I shall take up the first of these questions, namely, "What does it mean to maintain that the Tao 'forgets' Its undifferentiated oneness?"

As we've seen, for creation to occur, the Tao had to pay a twofold price: It had to "forget" Its inherent formlessness in order to experience Itself in and through Its multitudinous forms, and, as a result, It had to accept the illusion of dualism, Its sundry forms' seeming separation from one another.

"But surely," someone discerning soul will muse, "even granting a certain consistency in the claim that the Tao had to 'forget' Its formlessness if it is to take on form, how can we *ultimately* make sense of such a claim when the Tao is conceived of as a perfect, infinite, eternal, unique, and changeless Reality? For wouldn't such 'forgetfulness' imply that the Tao is imperfect, and if imperfect, then also finite, time-bound, non-unique, and changing? In short, wouldn't the Tao's absent-minded descent into the dualistic world of forms effectively contravene the Tao's fundamental Nature by relegating the Tao to the status of a mere creature?"

If the Tao's forgetfulness of Its formlessness seems a less than fathomable claim, I would offer two modest responses, one theological, the other logical. As to the modest theological response, I would begin by reminding (especially) my Christian readers that this is precisely the contention of most Christian theologians concerning Jesus's incarnation, namely, that the man Jesus, though God, had gradually to come to remember, to awaken to, his divinity.[7] This awakening Jesus unequivocally demonstrates in such statements as, "'I tell you most solemnly, before Abraham ever was, I Am'," and again, "'The Father and I are one'." (John 8:58;10:30, The Jerusalem Bible) The point of requiring Jesus to forget and then remember his divine Nature, say Christian theologians, is, before all else, to make meaningful Jesus's humanity and human experience. Otherwise, were Jesus fully conscious of his divinity from the start, this would mean that Jesus merely acted the part of a human being, that during his sojourn on Earth he only pretended to experience the fears, pain, sorrows, doubts, and confusion, as well as the pleasures, joys, hopes, exhilaration, and personal triumphs that are part and parcel of this earthly habitation.

Such a "play-acting" Jesus would render virtually meaningless Jesus's incarnation, and for two not insignificant reasons. For one thing, a Jesus who merely plays the part of a human being would severely undermine a hallowed Christian doctrine. The doctrine in question is that the primary reason God became human was to reveal the infinite depth of God's love for humanity, first, by the fact that an infinite God condescended to incarnate in a finite human form, and second, by the fact that God, in the person of Jesus, willingly died an excruciating death as ransom for a fallen humanity. For another thing, a Jesus who merely acts the part of a human being would make vacuous another sacrosanct Christian tenet, which is that Jesus's life is meant to serve as a singular model and source of hope for all human beings, as when Jesus proclaims: "In the world you will have trouble, but be brave: I have conquered the world." (John 16:33, The Jerusalem Bible) Clearly, a Jesus who manages to "conquer the world" while ever mindful of his divine status, whatever else he may be, can hardly be portrayed as an acceptable role model and source of inspiration for a struggling, fallible humanity.

If nothing else, the foregoing establishes that there is a theological precedent for the claim that the Tao "forgets" Its divinity, and thus Its formlessness, in the act of experiencing Itself in and through Its created forms. But this still leaves pending the question, raised above, of exactly how a perfect, infinite, eternal, unique, and changeless Tao can meaningfully be said to "forget" Its formless Nature in the act of creation, without thereby becoming Itself an imperfect, finite, temporal, non-unique, and changing created form? To which pending question I submit the following (not quite so) modest logical response.

By logical response, be it noted, I mean a reply that both makes sense and is consistent with what we already know about the Tao. In which regard, we learned in Chapter 2 that, given Its infinite Nature, the Tao must be at once transcendent of and immanent as Its creation. The only logical alternative, we saw, is to maintain that the Tao is either totally transcendent of or totally immanent as Its creation—either of which would-be alternatives clearly undoes the Tao's status as an infinite Reality, as well as negates both the Tao's divinity and creative activity.

Now, if the Tao must be at once transcendent of and immanent as Its creation, then, as we also saw, *qua* transcendent, the Tao retains Its identity as infinite, perfect, eternal, unique, and unchanging Reality. This means that, *qua* transcendent, the Tao is unaffected by, doesn't "lose Itself in," the limitations of Its creaturely Self-expressions. And *this*, as far as our present discussion is concerned, means that, *qua* transcendent, the Tao remains "fully aware of" Its divinity and formless Nature. However, *qua* immanent, the Tao is subject to the limitations of Its creaturely Self-expressions. Which, with specific respect to the discussion at hand, entails the Tao's "forgetfulness" of Its divinity and formless Nature as a condition of Its free decision to express Itself as

Its manifold of creaturely forms—as a condition, in other words, of Its voluntary "descent into the illusory realm of dualism." So that, just as it made sense to maintain that the infinite Tao must be both transcendent of and immanent as Its creation, even if we can't fully understand such divine simultaneity, it now seems no less reasonable to hold that the infinite Tao can "forget" Its formless divinity, just so long as we bear in mind that It does so solely in virtue of Its immanence, not in virtue of its transcendence. *Qua* transcendent, the Tao remains what It is, an infinite, perfect, eternal, unique, and changeless Reality that will ever be removed from and hence, not subject to, the spatio-temporal strictures of Its created order. For which reasons, it seems entirely within the bounds of logicality to aver that, notwithstanding Its "forgetfulness," the Creator Tao is not now, has never been, nor can ever be, a *complete* amnesiac!

Why Does the Tao Choose to Create?

Finally, let's consider our follow-up question: What would possess the Tao to create in the first place? And here again, we encounter a mystery no less profound than those we've previously discussed. But, as we noticed in Chapter 2, while such mystery-laden questions will ever exceed human comprehension, this isn't to say that they're *entirely* beyond human understanding, and thus that they're hopelessly meaningless questions. Indeed, the *Tao Te Ching* itself appears, however indirectly, to offer two possible reasons for the Tao's decision to create: the Tao's infinitely loving Nature and the Tao's desire to express Its infinite Nature in and through Its manifold forms.

As to the first of these possible reasons, that the Tao chooses to create as a function of Its infinitely loving Nature, I would first reiterate a major conclusion gleaned from my analysis of Poems 25 and 51 in Chapter 2, which is that the Tao is Infinite Love Itself. Now, few there are who would challenge the ancient maxim to the effect that unconditional love is by nature expansive, inclusive, giving, and communicative, never constrictive, exclusive, miserly, and non-communicative. Indeed, reflect, if you will, on your own love-filled moments. At such times do you not feel more alive, more creative, more open, more caring, more connected to, and desirous of sharing your life with, others? Most of us would have to admit, I think, that these are some of the more salient signs of that extraordinary thing called love, or at least, of unconditional love. But if so, if both in principle and from the personal experience of most of us, authentic love is of its very nature expansive, inclusive, giving, and communicative, and if the Tao *is* Love Itself, then it would seem that the Tao's choice to create, and thereby to express Itself in, through, and as Its myriad forms, is perfectly in keeping with a Reality that is Love Itself. And since, as we further concluded, the Tao's created forms are the Tao manifesting Itself in space and time, the love that moves the Tao to express Itself creatively is, when all is said and done, an act of *Self*-love on the Tao's part! In other words, creation, from the perspective of the *Tao Te Ching*, is, and can only be, born of the infinitely loving Tao's free decision to love Itself in and through Its multitudinous Self-expressions.[8]

Which brings us to the second reason the Tao may have chosen to create: Its desire to express Its infinite Nature in and through Its myriad created forms. But such a reason, we must confess, houses a rather large assumption to which the following question gives voice: What possible motivation would the Tao have to express Itself creatively, given that the Tao is *already an entirely perfect Reality?* To better appreciate the challenge to the Tao's creative activity this question poses, I would first point out that it does little good, by way of response, to argue that the infinite Tao, in light of Its transcendent/immanent relation to creation, *could* express Itself in and through Its multiplicity of created forms. To establish that the Tao *could* so express Itself, and even granting that the Tao *does* so express Itself, does not thereby establish why the Tao *would* desire to do so. Still begging an answer, then, is the even more fundamental question: Why would the all-perfect Tao even want to express Itself immanently, and hence imperfectly, in and through Its created forms? To which more fundamental question, I offer the following (more fundamental) reply.

And that is that the Tao's creative activity *stems motivationally from the Tao's infinite Nature Itself*. In support thereof, consider a passage from the *Tao Te Ching's* Poem 6:

> The Tao ... is empty yet inexhaustible,
> it gives birth to infinite worlds.

This passage, after intimating the Tao's formlessness ("The Tao is empty ...") as the source of the Tao's infinite creative *potential* ("... yet inexhaustible"), proceeds unequivocally to announce that the Tao has seen fit to *actualize* Its infinite potential ("... it gives birth to infinite worlds.")

This passage, I submit, serves two purposes. First, it clearly implies the Tao's desire to create by virtue of the fact that the Tao does create. And this because "The Tao follows only itself" (Poem 25), that is, is perfectly free, and thus under no external or internal compulsion to create. Whence, if the Tao does create, the Tao freely desires to do so, but only because the Tao views Its creative activity as desirable or good.

At the same time, the passage affords a clue as to why the Tao is motivated to create, that is, deems the act of creation a good and desirable thing. Creation is desirable precisely because the Tao is an infinite Reality. As such, it is entirely in keeping with Its Nature that the Tao, though all-perfect *qua* transcendent of creation, desires to express Itself immanently as well, by "giving birth to infinite worlds," and insofar, by engendering an infinite diversity of forms expressive of the infinite fecundity of Its Nature. Or look at the matter this way. *Qua* immanent, as a willing participant in the finite realm of created forms, the infinite Tao possesses infinite creative potential. If so, then it stands well to reason that, *qua* immanent, the Tao would desire to actualize Its infinite potential by giving birth to an infinite variety of created forms. True, these forms by which the Tao Self-expresses Itself are products of the Tao's voluntary "descent into the illusion of dualism," and so, are in themselves imperfect. But imperfection, which, on one level, we may regard as the "price" the Tao must pay to create, on another level, provides the opportunity, as it were, whereby the infinite Tao can experiment with and experience Itself in, through, and as an infinity of varied forms. Accordingly, I hold that, notwithstanding the Tao's perfection *qua* transcendent, it is neither contradictory nor absurd, and in truth, makes consummate good sense, to affirm that, *qua* immanent, the Tao desires to express Itself as Its created forms—to affirm, in short, that, in this respect at least, what the Tao *could do*, It *desires to do*.

Having in this chapter discussed the major consequences of the "Fall" from the sublimely elevated, and admittedly abstract, vantage point of the Tao Itself, it is now time to bring the Tao's "Fall" down to earth, so to speak, and to ask what principal, practical bearing the Tao's "Fall" has on Its creaturely Self-manifestations, in general, and Its human Self-manifestations, in particular. Such down-to-earth practicality shall be the subject of Chapter 4.

Notes

1. See Joseph Campbell, *Oriental Mythology: The Masks of God* (NY: Penguin Book, 1962), pp. 10–11.

2. In which regard, compare Genesis 1:27, wherein we read: "God created man in the image of himself, in the image of God he created him, male and female he created them." (The Jerusalem Bible)

3. Daniel Reid, *The Complete Book of Chinese Health and Healing* (NY: Barnes & Noble Books, 1994), p. 26.

4. See J.E. Bierlein, *Parallel Myths* (NY: Ballantine Books, 1994), pp. 100–104.

5. See Campbell, *Oriental Mythology*, p. 4.

6. See Genesis, Chapters1 and 2.

7. For an excellent study of Jesus's developing appreciation of his divinity, see John C. Haughy, S.J., *The Conspiracy of God: The Holy Spirit in Us* (NY: Image Books, 1976).

8. Aquinas suggests much the same love-motivated view of creation in *Summa Theologica*, Volume One, Question 44, Article 4; Question 45, Article 6; Question 47, Article 1 (NY: Benziger Brothers, Inc., 1946).

CHAPTER FOUR

The Downside of the Tao's "Fall" on Humanity

Can you coax your mind from its
wandering and keep to the original oneness?
Lao Tzu, Tao Te Ching, Poem 10

"When the Great Tao is Forgotten..."

The Tao's "Fall," we have seen, entails the Tao's "forgetfulness" of Its transcendent divinity, and hence, of Its formless Nature, as the condition of Its "descent into dualism," of Its Self-expression in and through Its panoply of created forms. The question that will occupy us in this chapter is, as promised, What practical bearing does the Tao's "Fall" have on Its human Self-expressions? To which Lao Tzu responds by first advising us of what we may take to be the "good news" of the *Tao Te Ching,* which is that "Each separate being in the universe," that is, each being that has lost sight of its true, loving Nature due to its illusory separation from the Tao, "returns to the common source." And why is this return "good news"? Because, answers Lao Tzu, "Returning to the source is serenity," that is, recovering our true, loving Nature through reunion with the Tao begets in us a "peace [that] is the highest value." (Poem 31). And peace, why is this the "highest value"? Because peace, by which Lao Tzu primarily means *inner peace,* is an infallible sign of love, and so of one's reunion with the Tao that *is* Love. Otherwise put, the "good news" of the *Tao Te Ching* is that each "Fallen," "each separate being," will recover its true, loving Nature when it returns to the Tao,* and in so doing, experience a "serenity" that is an unfailing indicator of its reconnection with, and hence, loving experience of, the Tao.

So much for the *Tao Te Ching's* "good news" (about which much more in Chapter 9). Now for its "quasi-bad news." Which is that, "If you don't realize [return to] the source," that is, if you don't recover your true, loving Nature by reuniting with the Tao, "you stumble in confusion and sorrow." (Poem 16) As to what Lao Tzu specifically understands by "confusion and sorrow" I shall have more to say later. Suffice it to say for now that Lao Tzu deems these unpleasant states of being the paramount downside issue of the Tao's "Fall" for Its human Self-expressions.

For Lao Tzu, then, our overriding task in life, given the Tao's willed "Fall," is to recover our true, loving Nature as the necessary condition of surmounting confusion and sorrow, and realizing the peace that is the surefire sign of our reunion with, and thus loving experience of, the Tao. But before we can better appreciate Lao Tzu's prescription for recovering our true Self, we'll need to backtrack somewhat and examine more closely why it is that our "forgetfulness" of the Tao yields the bitter harvest of confusion, sorrow, and want of inner peace that afflict humankind. Lao Tzu's answer, in general agreement with spiritual teachers of both Eastern and Western vintage, is that our illusory separation from the Tao spawns the spiritually perilous state of

---

*Actually, each separate being has *already* returned to the Tao, a point Lao Tzu implicitly makes when he writes, "Each separate being . . . *returns* to the source." Here, Lao Tzu speaks in the present tense, suggesting thereby that, from the eternal standpoint of "the eternal Tao," there is only the Now, the non-temporal moment. From an illusory temporal standpoint, which for the most part, is *our* standpoint, the return to the Tao has yet to occur. As we are presently locked in this temporal illusion, I shall continue to refer to the return as a work in progress, as a promissory future event that each and every one of us *will eventually realize*.

"attachment." So that, if we're to overcome confusion and sorrow, and thereby realize the peace that signals the recovery of our True Self and reconnection with the Tao, we will need to find a way out of our illusion-born attached condition. But why is it that Lao Tzu, in line with spiritual teachers past and present, views attachment as the supreme spiritual malady that he does? We catch an initial, cursory glimpse at why said teachers have so little regard for attachment when we realize, as Eastern religion scholars Swami Prabhavananda and Christopher Isherwood explain, that, "In general, mankind almost always acts with attachment; that is to say, with fear and desire. Desire for a certain result and fear that this result will not be obtained."[1] Thus, attachment amounts to desire qualified by fear, or, if you will, *fear-based* desire. Whenever someone ardently desires a certain outcome, say, a fulfilling relationship, or financial security, almost invariably, his desire will be attended by such fear-modes as doubt, worry, anxiety, and stress as to the realization of his fervently desired outcome. Evidently then, an attached life is less than conducive to a happy life. But before proceeding to discuss Lao Tzu's specific take on attachment, I shall consider in some further detail why an attached life is inimical to a happy life, and more precisely, why an attached life is detrimental to both our psychological and spiritual well-being.

The Downside of Attachment on Our Psychological and Spiritual Well-Being

The *immediate* psychological toll the attached life can take on a person is all-too evident. As was noted, to be caught in the throes of attachment is to live one's life beset by fears that cannot but undermine one's psychological (mental and emotional) well-being. A concrete case in point: an attached student preparing to take an exam. The student greatly desires an A grade on the exam, but being attached to results, his desire is plagued by the fear that his exam-taking efforts will not turn out well, or at least not as well as he had hoped. While studying for the exam, the student's concern as to the outcome saps his energy and makes it all the more difficult to concentrate and retain the material. He arrives for the exam, probably after several restless, if not sleepless, nights. He takes the exam—also in an attached state, which means, of course, that he, perhaps even more than ever, struggles with fear-begotten distractions. Well, let's suppose that our student, upon completing the exam, harbors some hope that he has done well. Will this serve to assuage his fears and misgivings? Unfortunately, the answer is almost certainly no. And why? Because, as long as he abides in fear as to the exam's outcome, *he will conjure up fear-born reasons to believe in an unsuccessful outcome!* "Perhaps I'm only kidding myself," he may wonder. Or, "There were several true and false questions that were kind of iffy. And that essay—did I manage to get across all the major points, and to do so in a manner agreeable to fusty Professor X?" And so it obsessively goes. As it happens, our student receives the desired "A" for his troubles. Is this now the merciful end of the story, as far as this student is concerned? As you doubtless well realize, not by a long shot! In fact, it is only the beginning, so to speak. For now, our still-attached student will soon be visited by a plague of further worries, doubts, anxieties, in a word, fears, surrounding future exams. Perhaps he "lucked out" this time. Will he be able to "keep up" this level of pressurized academic achievement? Should he "bomb" his next exam, will Professor X think any less of him? perhaps suspect him of having cheated on his previous exam? and like disquieting reflections. Moreover, almost certainly, our student's attached frame of mind won't be confined to taking college exams. Unfortunately, for this student, as for all practitioners of attachment, life writ large becomes one big, onerous, and inexorable "test," a test that, precisely because he is beset with deep-seated, chronic worries, doubts, anxieties, in a word, fears, he has no hope of ever really "passing."

But beyond such immediate attachment-spawned psychological woes, the attached person inevitably finds himself bewitched, bothered, and beleaguered by an undercurrent of desperation. And this because the attached person, who abides in the illusion of separation from the Source, as we've seen, fails to appreciate that it is only the infinite Source, the all-perfect Good, that can truly, fully, and endlessly satisfy him. For this reason, the attached person will look to finite, transient goods—in the main, wealth, power, success, and pleasure—as the source of his happiness, in a futile quest after fulfillment, a fulfillment that will ever elude him.

And, as if this were not a sufficiently bleak state of affairs, the pertinaciously attached individual is destined for things bleaker still. For, the longer he persists in seeking fulfillment in the finite-transient goods of this mortal realm, the greater his desperation becomes; and as his desperation mounts, so too does its issue, the likes of frustration, restlessness, perplexity, anger, discouragement, anxiety, depression, and even despair.

Last but by no means least, caught in the vise grip of these and like melancholy mental and emotional conditions, an individual cannot but sink ever deeper into a state of unremitting preoccupation with and fixation upon himself, to the exclusion of other selves, and most notably, the Supreme Self, apart from Whom there is no final respite from the contagion of desperation and its consequent mentally and emotionally debilitating progeny.

And so, a life bedeviled by fear as to the outcome of things, a waning of energy and concentrative power, an existence fraught with desperation, begetting in its turn further mental, emotional, and often physical maladies, all culminating in a state of extreme self-absorption and a deflecting of one's attention from the Infinite Source, the sole Good that can put to rest one's perpetual unrest—such are the unhappy psychological and spiritual prospects awaiting the habitual practitioner of the attached life.

Lao Tzu: Attachment as Ultimate Source of Confusion and Sorrow

So far in this chapter I have made the following points concerning attachment: (1) that attachment, the product of our illusory separation from the Tao, is the proximate source of humankind's confusion, sorrow, and dearth of inner peace, (2) that attachment is consequently what we need to overcome if we are to transcend confusion and sorrow, and realize the peace that signals the recovery of our true, loving

Nature and reunion with the Tao, and (3) that attachment amounts to *fear-based* desire, which is to say, attachment's distinguishing mark, that which sets it apart from other modes of desire, is that it is desire laden with fear as to the outcome of an event.

The question that will occupy us in this section is whether Lao Tzu concurs in the foregoing account of the origin, causative influence, and nature of attachment. That he does so concur consider, to begin with, the following passages from the *Tao Te Ching*, the first of which reads:

> The Master … is detached from all things;
> that is why she is one with them. (Poem 7)

That is, if detachment, attachment's opposite number, is the sign and condition of union with all that is, and in particular, with the Tao, then it is clear that Lao Tzu cannot but regard attachment as the sign and condition of disunion from all that is, and in particular, from the Tao.

The next set of passages, taken as a whole, more expressly illustrate Lao Tzu's agreement as to the fear-based character of attachment, as well as his acceptance of the traditional view that attachment, born of the illusion of separation from the Tao, is the proximate source of humankind's problems, and thus that attachment must be overcome if we are to transcend these problems and experience the inner peace that is the infallible sign of our reunion with the Tao:

The first passage states:

> Fear … arises from thinking of the self. (Poem 13)

Here, Lao Tzu alludes to our separation from the Tao, as well as from all manifestations of the Tao, by alluding to the belief in a separate "self," over and against other distinct and separate "selves" (a belief we've previously and more generally designated "dualism.") This belief in a separate "self" generates the primal emotion of "fear" ("*Fear* … arises from thinking of the self.") But why fear? Because to the extent that one views another as separate, and so, as "other," one cannot but view this other as unknown. And insofar as one views this other as unknown, one will perforce view this other as dangerous, and specifically, as a threat to one's "self." Finally, to the degree that one views this other as a threat to one's self, one will, and can only, relate to this other as someone or something to be feared. Whence it is that, in the end, "Fear . . . arises from thinking of the self [as separate from other selves, including the Supreme Self, the Tao].".

On the other hand,

> When we don't see the self as self,
> what do we have to fear? (Poem 13)

When we transcend the illusory separate self, fear, the basis of attachment, vanishes. But we can only transcend the illusory separate self, which is to say, the illusion of dualism, by overcoming our fear-based attachments:

> There is no greater illusion than fear . . .
> *Whoever can see through all fear*
> *will always be safe*. (Poem 46) [Italics added]

In other words, as one conquers her fear-based attachments, and thereby masters the illusion of dualism (belief in a separate "self"), she becomes

> centered in the Tao [and]
> can go where she wishes, without danger.
> She perceives the universal harmony,
> even amid great pain,
> because she has found peace in her heart. (Poem 35)

For Lao Tzu, then, the way that leads us beyond the twin downside consequences of the Tao's willful "Fall," confusion and sorrow, and into the peace that signals the recovery of our true, loving Nature and reconnection with the Tao, is a way wherein we must confront and then conquer dualism's prime effect, our fear-born attachments.

Attachment as Antithetical to the Tao's Loving Nature

But if it is clear why attachment is psychologically and spiritually uncongenial to our pursuit of the Tao, Lao Tzu implicitly suggests a yet more fundamental reason for attachment's uncongeniality herein, a reason that hearkens back to our discussion (in Chapter 2) of the Tao's essentially loving Nature. There, we saw that the Tao is unconditionally loving, *because the Tao is Love Itself*. For this reason, we further saw, the "True Nature" of creatures, even of *human* creatures!, being of the selfsame substance as the Tao, is essentially and naturally loving.

Also recall that fear is the defining feature of attachment, in that attachment amounts to fear-based desire for a certain result, and that attachment is dualism's—the illusion of separation from the Tao and the Tao's created Self-manifestations—primary effect.

Bearing all this in mind, we may now proceed to explicate Lao Tzu's implicit, more fundamental reason for regarding attachment as inimical to our quest after the Tao. And that would be that attachment, rooted as it is in fear, is diametrically opposed to the Tao's essentially loving Nature, since that which separates us from the Tao can in no way be attributed to, much less identified with, the Nature of the Tao. Which effectively means that (1) fear and (true) love are opposites, (2) fear is antithetical both to the Tao that is Love and to the true, loving Nature of the Tao's created Self-manifestations, (3) the more one abides in fear, the less will one love others, experience one's true, loving Nature, and realize union with the Tao, and (4) the more one abides in love, the more will one love others, experience one's true, loving Nature, and realize union with the Tao. In sum, then, attachment is *the* impediment to our reconnection with the Tao, the recovery of our true, loving Nature, the conquering of the twin diseases of confusion and sorrow, and the realization of the peace that passeth understanding—because it fixates us in a state of fear that is absolutely and unremittingly opposed to the Tao that is Love.

Is the Tao's "Fall" Worth It?

Before exiting this chapter, it might be well to raise a question that may have occurred to the Reader: to wit, in light of the downside consequences of the Tao's willful "Fall," which Lao Tzu summarizes as confusion, sorrow, and the waning of inner peace, was the "Fall" really worth it? Even more to the point: Was the amount and degree of suffering wrought by the Tao's desire to experiment with and experience Itself in, through, and as Its innumerable created forms (see Chapter 3) worth it?

In posing this question, we submit a version of a question that, for most, is *the* question: Why do we suffer? As we've noticed, there are certain questions, especially with respect to the Source, that defy a comprehensive or complete answer, and this certainly qualifies as one of those questions. Even so, and as we've also noticed, this isn't to say that we can't supply an answer that, though beyond our comprehension, still makes sense, and in particular, that is consistent with what we already know about, in this case, the Tao. But so as to prepare the way for my ventured answer to the question, Why has the Tao seen fit to embody Itself as Its manifold created forms, notwithstanding the amount and degree of "confusion" (error, ignorance, misunderstanding, doubt, delusion, misguided and/or failed aspirations and goals) and "sorrow" (physical pain and disease, psychological pain and disease, cruelty, violence, injustice) that are the necessary, albeit temporary, consequences of Its creative decision? I shall take the somewhat circuitous route of first suggesting why, in my opinion, typically Western answers to the worthwhileness of suffering in relation to God may be, when all is said and done, less acceptable than Lao Tzu's (implied) answer.

A Fundamental Problem with Western Attempts to Justify God in the Face of Suffering

To begin with, recall that, for the *Tao Te Ching*, created forms *are* the Tao Self-expressing Itself. This is a point on which, as I indicated in Chapter 1, the *Tao Te Ching* differs markedly from Judeo-Christian and Islamic theology. For the latter, creatures are by definition finite,

God, by definition infinite. Moreover, creatures are deemed to be eternally beholden to and dependent upon God for their very existence. Primarily for these reasons, Western theologians argue, creatures are by nature eternally and absolutely distinct from God, and it is a sheer contradiction, not to mention the gravest of blasphemies, to hold that the finite creature is, or can ever hope to be, the selfsame as the Infinite Creator.

Working as most Western theologians do from a "separatist" perspective concerning God and creatures, the question, Why, given the amount and degree of suffering in the world, did God still see fit to create?[2] becomes, I submit, more problematical. "More problematical," I say, because, by regarding God as radically distinct from creation, theologians' answers to the problem of suffering, however brilliant, insightful and interesting, are inextricably shadowed by the theological principle that God, for whatever good and noble reasons (e.g., creating free and responsible beings, the possibility of eternal happiness in heaven), yet permits His creatures to endure a great deal of suffering, *while God remains personally and experientially aloof therefrom*. My point, in other words, is not that, given a "separatist" theological principle, one can't devise a respectable justification of God's goodness and power *vis-à-vis* suffering; my point is rather that any such proffered justification becomes less palatable, so to speak, in view of God's radical distinction from, and therefore, non-experience of, creatures' suffering.

An Immanence-Based Objection to the View That God Doesn't Suffer

I can think of two possible objections to the above view that God does not personally partake of creatures' suffering. One such objection might appeal to the fact that mainstream Western theology, as we've noticed, readily grants God's immanence in, as well as transcendence of, creation. This being the case, It may be said that God's non-participation in creatures' suffering refers to God's transcendence of creation, not to God's immanence in creation. *Qua* immanent, God participates in creation, and if so, cannot but experientially share in creatures' suffering.

As compelling as this objection might seem, it comes up short when we recall that, for most Western theologians, God is immanent in creation as the eternally sustaining and all-powerful Cause of creatures' existence. On this theology, God's immanence in creation amounts to God's ongoing activity of bestowing existence on finite creatures. This means, in the words of Aquinas, that

> God exists in everything, not indeed as part of their substance or as an accident [a feature of a substance, e.g., color, size, shape], but as an agent is present to that in which its action is taking place.[3]

That is, just as an agent, say, a lady wielding a knife, causes an effect, say, sliced havarti cheese, but is, of course, not herself part of the sliced havarti cheese-effect, so it is that God, as ongoing Agent Cause of creatures' existence,[4] is responsible for creatures' existence, without Himself being part of, much less identified with, creatures. Evidently, then, in spite of the Western theological doctrine of God's immanence in creation, in its concern to insure God's distinction from creation, Western theology, at the same time, makes it abundantly clear that God, however else He may participate in creation,[5] does not Himself personally partake of or experience creatures' sufferings.

An Incarnation-Based Objection to the View That God Doesn't Suffer

A second objection to the claim that Western theology absolutely denies God's personal experience of suffering reintroduces a point made in Chapter 3. There, among other things, I mentioned the Christian doctrine of the Incarnation, the view that God sent Christ, who is both God and man, to demonstrate His love for the finite world, as well as to give hope to and ultimately to redeem a Fallen humanity through Christ's intercessory sacrificial death.

Now, to believe that God loves and is concerned with His suffering world, and even that God allowed Christ to suffer for the sake of the world, does not in itself show that God is experientially involved in His suffering world. To argue that God does so suffer, given the Incarnation, requires a more precise look at what the Incarnation is doctrinally about. More precisely, then, the doctrine asserts that Christ unites two natures, human and divine, in one person. Christian theology readily concedes the mysterious character of this doctrine, in that, for normal experience, a nature, say, human nature, doesn't exist in its own right, but rather as embodied in an individual, in this case, an individual person, who shares his or her human nature with other persons. In other words, for normal experience, where there is a nature, there is an individual who embodies that nature, be it an individual person, an individual tree, an individual cat, or an individual whatever. Whence the mystery of the Incarnation: though there be two natures, human and divine, their union results not in two persons (as we, given our normal experience, would expect), but in one person, namely, the person of the God-man, Christ.[6]

If we allow the Incarnation's affirmation of the unity of both human and divine natures in the one person of Christ, this not only demonstrates God's awareness of and compassion for a suffering world (as noted in Chapter 3); even more significantly, it seems also to demonstrate at least this much: that, insofar as the human Jesus suffered, God no less suffered. For if the human and divine natures verily constitute one person, then does it not stand well to reason that what happens to the one, happens to the other? Else, how can Christianity insist that the human and divine natures form a unity, that they constitute one, and only one, person?

Anyone of a mind to offer this faith-based doctrine as evidence that God does, or at least did, truly suffer, would appear to have logic (consistency in reasoning) on her side. Furthermore, beyond the logicality of her position, she might point to the "normal person," as a union of body and soul/mind, by way of further, *analogical* support for her contention that God must suffer, if Christ is truly a person. More clearly, she might point to the experiential fact that a "normal person" suffers as a *whole* person. This is evidenced by the fact that we usually say, when suffering, "I'm in pain," or perhaps, "My body is hurting" (which expression, though explicitly pointing to the body as the source of suffering, implicitly subsumes the body under a larger identity, namely, a person, as indicated by the adjective "My," the possessive form of the first-person personal pronoun "I.") Nor, be it noted, does it discredit the view that a "normal person" suffers as a whole to adduce instances of the phenomenon of "mind over matter," where persons, such as certain practitioners of yoga, have been known to transcend physical suffering by placing themselves in an altered state of consciousness. For, in such mind-over-matter cases, instead of the whole person experiencing physical pain, *the whole person has presumably developed the ability to alter her consciousness so as not to experience physical pain*. In other words, in the former case, a person suffers because she is united body and soul/mind; in the latter case, a person transcends suffering because the unity of body and soul/mind enables certain adepts to control their bodily states by controlling/altering their mental states. Thus, the phenomenon of mind-over-matter, far from refuting the contention that it is the whole person who suffers, actually lends indirect support to the whole-person-suffering contention. And with this challenge to the whole-person-suffering equation out of the way, we are seemingly even more within our rights in affirming that, if, as the Incarnation doctrine holds, the person of Christ (in some mysterious way) expresses a perfect unity of human nature and divine nature, then insofar as the human being, Jesus, suffered, the divine being, God, no less suffered.

I readily concede the logicality and analogical evidentiality of the above Incarnationally based argument in behalf of the claim that God personally experiences suffering. Unfortunately, it doesn't seem that Christian theologians are likewise disposed to accept any such logically and analogically based conclusion. In which ill-disposed respect, consider the very first clear-cut statement of the doctrine of the Incarnation, given by Pope Leo the Great (d. 461). After declaring that human nature and divine nature are united in the person of Christ, Pope Leo adds that

> Each of the two natures performs the functions proper to it in communion with the other: the Word [divine Nature] does what pertains to the Word and the flesh [human nature] what pertains to the flesh.[7]

The thrust of this citation, for our present purposes, seems to be that, despite the union of human and divine natures in Christ, they each have their own specific and proper spheres of activities and involvements. The activities and involvements proper to human nature per se are not those proper to divine nature per se. And among the activities and involvements clearly proper to human nature per se is the activity of and involvement in suffering. If so, then it would seem that Pope Leo is tacitly endorsing the position that, though Christ is at once God and man, it is only as man that Christ suffers, not as God.

And what Pope Leo leaves implicitly stated, Thomas Aquinas, without question the most influential of Incarnation thinkers, argues explicitly. After citing St. Ambrose's view that God can't be a creature, because "God has a simple [formless] not a composite Nature," Aquinas proceeds to explain that

> We must not say absolutely that Christ is a *creature* or *less than the Father* [God]; but with a qualification, viz. *in His human nature*. But such things as could not be considered to belong to the Divine Person in Itself may be predicated simply of [attributed to] Christ by reason of His human nature; thus we say simply that Christ suffered, died, and was buried; even as in corporeal and human beings . . .[8]

What Aquinas's remarks boil down to is this: Christ as God, in His divine nature, is not a creature, and hence does not, indeed, cannot, suffer. However, Christ, as man, in his human nature, is a creature, and hence is susceptible to suffering even unto death.[9] And so we see that despite the fact that Christian theologians insist on the absolute unity of human and divine natures in the person of Christ; and despite the fact that their insistence herein seems logically to require a communion of experiences between Christ's human and divine natures; despite these things, Christian theologians are no less insistent that there exists a radical distinction or *dis*unification between God and creature, thereby insuring that God, however else He may be involved in the goings-on of His creatures, does not, indeed, cannot, participate experientially in their suffering.

The Worthwhileness of the Tao's Decision to Create, According to the *Tao Te Ching*

In the foregoing (long-winded) discussion, I was at pains to show that Western theologians, however else they may endeavor to justify God in the face of suffering, can't do so by appealing to God's experiential involvement in creatures' suffering. Neither an argument from God's immanence nor from the Christian doctrine of the Incarnation will serve to establish that God is "one of us," when it comes to suffering. In the Western theological scheme of things, God is, can only be, and will e'er remain radically distinct from creation, in general, and suffering creation, in particular.

That Western theologians can't appeal to God's experiential involvement in creatures' suffering, I said, makes any such effort on their part to justify God in the face of evil "more problematical." And why? Because whatever such theologians say in God's defense, however well-devised and plausible their justifications may be, their justificatory efforts are nonetheless hounded by the theological tenet that God remains personally and experientially removed from His creatures' suffering. The situation here is roughly analogous to a father who, for good and noble and even loving reasons, allows his children to endure enormous suffering, while he himself remains personally removed from and unmoved by their suffering. What I am trying to say, in other words, is that there is something incongruous and unfitting about a theology in which, on the one hand, a God Who is Love lovingly begets and cares for His creation, and yet, on the other hand, remains radically distinct from His creatures, in general, and His creatures' suffering, in particular.

The doctrine of immanence in the *Tao Te Ching*, you will recall, asserts not only that the Tao is in Its created forms, as Western theologians generally grant; even more fundamentally, it asserts that the Tao actually *is* Its created forms. To be sure, the *Tao Te Ching* upholds as well the infinite Tao's transcendence of creation, and insofar, Its "distance" from creation. *Qua* immanent, however, or insofar as the Tao *is* Its created forms, there can be no radical distinction between the Tao and creation. And if, immanently speaking, no radical distinction exists between the Tao and creation, then this can only mean that the Tao is personally, experientially involved in Its creation, and therefore, that the Tao has willingly elected, for a time at least, to suffer as the price of its creative experience/experiment on this dual plane of existence.

I suggest, then, that the amount and degree of suffering wrought by the Tao's "Fall," Its decision to create, is made more palatable, if not entirely understandable, in light of the *Tao Te Ching's* view that creatures are the Tao expressing and experiencing Itself in space and time. Such a view is more palatable, I believe, for at least two reasons. For one thing, it makes it easier to accept the worthwhileness of suffering if we can accept a view that says, in effect, the Tao, the supreme Source of all that is, has nonetheless seen fit to create, despite the amount and degree of suffering the Tao, embodied as Its created forms, is prepared to endure. Such a view is more apt to instill hope and to foster the conviction that there actually is a point to suffering. For if the Tao that is Love is willing to undergo suffering in and through Its myriad Self-expressions, then—and unless the Tao is a Supreme Masochist!—we have no reason to doubt that the Tao's willingness to experience suffering must be well worth it.

A second, related reason why suffering is perhaps more palatable in the *Tao Te Ching's* scheme of things is the well-recognized fact that it is immensely easier to bear up under suffering when we know that we are not alone in our suffering, when we know that someone has more or less personally experienced what we are going through, and especially when we know that, because we *are* the Tao, everything that we are experiencing is precisely what the Tao is experiencing!

Primarily for these reasons, I submit that anyone endeavoring to argue the worthwhileness of the Source's decision to create will have an easier, albeit not an easy, time of it if he adopts the *Tao Te Ching's* perspective on creation.

Which brings us to the next question that Lao Tzu effectively asks: What has been the all but universal human response to the confusion, suffering, cruelty, violence, want of peace, and so on, that are the downside issue of the Tao's Fall? To which question the all-but universal answer has been that human nature, left to its own devices, can't really be trusted, and therefore that human beings require the structure, discipline and guidance afforded especially by the rule of law, moral standards, and religious principles, if they are to cherish any hope of surviving, much less leading good, meaningful, and truly spiritual lives.

Lao Tzu, as we've observed, rejects any such denigrating view of human nature. But no less does he reject law, morality, and religion as *ultimate* liberators of humankind from the dour triad of confusion, sorrow, and want of inner peace. If interested in why Lao Tzu finds law, morality, and even religion unsatisfactory as final answers to humankind's woes, may I recommend your perusal of Chapter 5?

Notes

1. See Appendix II, "The Gita and War," in *The Song of God: Bhagavad-Gita*, trans., Swami Prabhavananda and Christopher Isherwood (N.Y: Mentor, 1944), p. 137. It should be noted that an age-old misconception continues to haunt the notions of attachment and detachment. I allude to the tendency among both Eastern and Western spiritual thinkers, past and present, to equate attachment with desire, and detachment with sheer desirelessness. In Chapter 8, among other things, I shall show why these common, longstanding renderings of detachment and attachment are far from adequate, as well as argue (1) for Prabhavananda and Isherwood's characterization of attachment as fear-based desire and (2) for a more adequate rendering of detachment. For an interesting recent discussion of the ambiguity surrounding the notions of detachment and attachment, see Joel J. Kupperman, *Classic Asian Philosophy: A Guide to the Essential*

Texts (N.Y: Oxford University Press, 2001), pp. 30–38, 52–55, 62, 121, 139–40, 151.

2. In the West, the theological area that fields such questions has traditionally been termed "theodicy," to wit, a reasoned attempt to salvage God's goodness and power in the face of physical suffering and moral evil. The three most prominent Christian spokespersons herein are St. Irenaeus (ca. 125–202), St. Augustine (354–430), and St. Thomas Aquinas (1225–1274).

3. St.Thomas Aquinas, *Summa Theologica*, Volume One, Question 8, Article 1, Reply (NY: Benziger Brothers, Inc., 1946).

4. *Ibid*.

5. This, of course, is not to suggest that Western theology denies that God loves, cares for, and wisely guides His creatures. Indeed, this is exactly what the Western theological doctrine of Providence maintains (in which regard see, Thomas Aquinas, *Summa Theologica*, Volume One, Question 22). I am simply suggesting that, God's Providence notwithstanding, Western theology strenuously argues that God, *qua* God, can't experientially participate in creatures' suffering.

6. See St.Thomas Aquinas, *Summa Theologica*, Volume Three, Questions 2–6, 17–19 (NY: Benziger Brothers, Inc, 1948).

7. Cited by Richard P. McBrien, *Catholicism* (San Francisco, CA: Harper & Row, 1981), p. 454.

8. St. Thomas Aquinas, *Summa Theologica*, Volume Three, Question 16, Article 8 (NY: Benziger Brothers, Inc, 1948).

9. For Aquinas's account of the precise ways in which the human Christ suffered, see *Ibid.*, Question14, Articles 1–3: Question 15, Articles 4–7; and Question 16, Article 8.

CHAPTER FIVE

Lao Tzu on Morality, Religion, and Law

The Tao is beyond all value…

Lao Tzu, Tao Te Ching, Poem 62

Lao Tzu on Morality, Religion, and Law

As noted in Chapter 4, Lao Tzu doesn't believe that the triad of law, morality, and religion represent ultimate solutions to the sorrow, confusion, and dearth of inner peace that afflict the great majority of humankind.[1] Why is Lao Tzu so dubious of this ancient triad's capacity to liberate human beings from their mental, emotional, and physical shackles? Actually, Lao Tzu's answer to this question may be implicitly gleaned from the preceding chapters. However, his answer is much too important not to hear him out explicitly. And nowhere does he more succinctly articulate why he deems law, morality, and religion incapable of resolving the world's woes, I submit, than in the first four lines of Poem 18:

> When the great Tao is forgotten,
> goodness and piety appear.
> When the body's intelligence declines,
> cleverness and knowledge step forth.

I shall consider each of these lines in turn, beginning with…

"When the great Tao is forgotten ..."

Here, Lao Tzu evidently refers to the Tao's "Fall," the main consequence of which, as we've seen, is attachment or *fear-based* desire, the proximate cause of the unholy trinity of confusion, sorrow, and a want of inner peace. That attachment is the proximate cause of this unhallowed trinity is due not only to the fact that a life beset by fear inevitably spawns unpleasant and unwholesome physical, psychological and spiritual conditions. Even more fundamentally, attachment is the proximate cause of our tripartite woes because it perpetuates the illusion of our separation from the Tao. More to the point, rooted as it is in fear, the antithesis of love, attachment fosters the illusory belief that we are cut off from the Tao that is Love, thereby causing us to lose sight of, to "forget," our true, loving Nature, to forget, in other words, that our "True Nature" (Poem 65)*is* the Tao.

The principal upshot of our forgetfulness of the Tao, rooted as it is in the fear-based desire that is attachment, then, is this: insofar as we regard ourselves as separate from the Tao that is Love, and thereby lose sight of our true, loving Nature, our natural capacity to act lovingly is diminished. But when our natural capacity to act lovingly is diminished, states Lao Tzu,

"Goodness and piety appear."

In this laconic phrase Lao Tzu alludes to the three most prominent and persistent "authority figures" to which people of all cultures have historically turned: morality, religion, and law. It is primarily to these three, Lao Tzu insists, that we look, whether consciously or not, for our understanding of and motivation to live our lives in accord with "goodness," and specifically, for our understanding of and motivation to be good persons and to lead a good life, when and to the extent that "the great Tao is forgotten." Now, as has been duly noted, Lao Tzu is firmly of the opinion that these would-be authorities are not, indeed, can never be, legitimate and effective sources of guidance, inspiration, courage, and purpose once "the great Tao is forgotten," a view he expresses, for example, in the following excerpts:

> Throw away morality and justice, and people will do
> the right thing.(Poem 19)
>
> I let go of the law, and people become honest...
> I let go of religion, and people become serene.
> (Poem 57)

The fundamental problem, already indicated in the previous section, is that, as we abide in the illusion of our separateness from the Tao, we become mired in attachment, in fear-based desire, and thus experience a diminution of our natural, Tao-given capacity to act in a loving manner. Moreover, as we experience a diminution of our capacity to act in a naturally loving manner, we cannot but regard ourselves as unwhole, incomplete, inadequate, and unworthy. But when we so regard ourselves, "... we no longer trust ourselves, and begin to depend upon authority." (Poem 72) That is to say, when we "no longer trust ourselves," we give our power away, put power outside ourselves, primarily and inevitably by inventing, Lao Tzu maintains, external authority figures, chief among which are morality, religion, and law.

In other words, the existence, and especially the predominance, of morality, religion, and law, as far as Lao Tzu is concerned, is an unfailing sign that, to a greater or lesser extent, we have lost sight of our true, loving Nature. As such, the great irony is that to live a truly moral, religious, and law-abiding life is no guarantee whatsoever that we are living a truly loving life. In fact, if anything, insofar as individuals are votaries of morality, religion, and law, they will lack the inner love-based strength and conviction to live their lives in accord with the very moral norms, religious principles, and legal constraints they espouse!—a point Lao Tzu tersely underscores when he states:

> Try to make people moral [or religious or law-abiding],
> and you lay the groundwork for vice. (Poem 58)

More to the point, we "lay the groundwork for vice" because, deficient in the unifying power of love, and thus to that extent caught in the clutches of a disunifying attachment, we cannot but regard "others" as objects of fear. So regarding others, we cultivate the conviction that we, and we alone, are sole possessors of the holy grail of moral, religious, and legal truth as to what constitutes right action and the good life. From this, we find it all too easy, indeed, even "necessary," to sit in self-righteous judgment of those not so possessed of the truth. And from this, it is but a short further step to be moved to take "just" action against these less than righteous "others," even action unto violence. All of which Lao Tzu undoubtedly has in mind when he observes:

> The moral man does something,
> and when no one responds
> he roles up his sleeves and uses force. (Poem 38)

The final unfortunate stage of a life short on love-based inner strength and long on attachment-born fear Lao Tzu puts as follows:

> When morality [or religion or law] is lost, there is ritual.
> Ritual is the husk of true faith,
> the beginning of chaos. (Poem 38)

When, and to the extent that, our lives are unsuffused with love, not only will we lack the inner strength and conviction ("true faith") to conform our lives to moral, religious, and legal precepts; our efforts to conform our lives to moral, religious, and legal precepts will amount to little more than empty "ritual," to perfunctorily going through the moral, religious, or legal motions, in the misguided belief that being morally respectable, religiously orthodox, or legally exact renders us truly good and even loving individuals. And with this final delusion well in place, the situation is now ripe for the onset of "chaos"—for the loss of even the feeble, beclouded guidance and comfort afforded by morality, religion, and law, and for the "gaining" of a life increasingly in the throes of that triad of attachment-begotten maladies: sorrow, confusion, and a dearth of inner peace.

But when, and to the extent that, we lose our natural capacity to act lovingly, we equally lose our natural, intuitive connection to the Tao, a loss Lao Tzu figuratively suggests when next he writes:

"When the body's intelligence declines ..."

The Reader will recall the abbreviated mention of intuition at the end of Chapter 1. There, among other things, the point was made that the act of intuition is generally signaled by certain attending physiological responses, and so is often indirectly referred to in terms of various bodily based metaphors. I submit, then, that Lao Tzu's reference to "the body's intelligence" is just such a metaphor for the act of intuition.

I broached the topic of intuition at the conclusion of Chapter 1 so as to call attention to Lao Tzu's view that the conceptual mode of knowing the Tao must be transcended in favor of intuitive knowing, as well as to introduce in a preliminary way what intuitive knowing is and how it differs from conceptual knowing. As to the inadequacy of conceptual knowing, we saw that such knowing, for all its grandeur, is nevertheless a categorical, and therefore, dualistic mode of knowing. But as the Tao is by nature formless, and therefore a decidedly *non*-dual Reality, conceptual knowing, though at its best capable of meaningful affirmations about the Tao, is, and will ever be, cognitively unequal to the task of understanding the Tao. It is primarily for this reason that Lao Tzu, in agreement with virtually all spiritual sages, past and present, contends that "normal" conceptual knowing must be surpassed in favor of intuitive knowing, if our "minds [are to] be at one with the Tao." (Poem 21)

But precisely what is it about intuitive knowing that allows our "minds [to] be at one with the Tao"? The answer to this all-important question requires that we take a closer look at what intuition is and how it differs from conceptual knowing. In which regard, I suggested in Chapter 1 that intuition amounts to a direct and immediate experience of, and insight into, a person, place, thing, or event. As such, intuitive knowing differs markedly from the categorical and dualistic view of reality that are the hallmarks of conceptual knowing. Rather than discerning a person, place, thing, or event generally, inferentially, and impersonally, *à la* conceptual knowing, intuitive knowing apprehends a person, place, thing, or event particularly, immediately, and personally. The first two aspects of intuitive knowing, particularity and immediacy, refer to the process by which the intuiter grasps a given person, place, thing, or event, namely, by a direct insight into something pertaining peculiarly to a person, place, thing, or event. The last aspect of intuitive knowing, its personal nature, pertains to the intuiter's personal response to an intuitive experience. Briefly put, we may say that intuitive knowing engages the intuiter *as a whole person*. Less briefly put, we may say that intuitive knowing affects the knower, not in the impersonal manner of conceptual knowing, but rather primarily in an emotive, and hence, highly personal manner. Which is why intuition is not uncommonly designated by such bodily based metaphors as "gut knowledge" and "heart knowledge," and why Lao Tzu sees fit to allude to intuition via the more generic bodily based metaphor, "the body's intelligence."

Of course, given the particular, immediate, and personal nature of intuitive knowing, a "drawback" to such knowing is its subjectivity, the fact that it lacks the evidential objectivity of conceptual knowing. When, for example, someone enters a vacant room and claims a "gut feeling" about certain unpleasant events that transpired there in the past, without any apparent evidence to back up her feeling, we see in bold relief the conflict that often arises between these two modes of knowing. When one intuits something, she immediately sees/feels that, in this particular situation, such and such is the case. No objective evidence, at least at the time, can be offered in support of one's intuition.

Furthermore, if the particularity, immediacy, and personal character of intuitive knowing renders it unsusceptible to objective, evidential verification, this is only to say that intuitive knowing can't be communicated through normal conceptual channels. Normal conceptual knowing, as I've noted, communicates by categorizing reality, as when we say "This plant is a tree," "That cat is female," "The lady is a soldier," and so on. When we categorize reality, we subsume distinct individuals, such as the aforementioned plant, cat, and lady, under a given class, in this case, "tree," "female," and "soldier," respectively. In so doing, we mentally disengage from those features that render individuals unique, such as physical appearance, personality, temperament, talents and interests. Otherwise put, when we categorize reality, we reduce a concrete individual to features that are common to *all* the individual members of its class, as when we refer to an individual as "male," "carpenter," "republican," or what have you. But this categorizing or generalizing of and disengagement from individuals' unique features is the price we must pay if we are to have a common language, since that which is unique about individuals, being immune to conceptualization, is *ipso facto* immune to categorization, and hence, to a common language.

But perhaps no mode of intuitive knowing more graphically illustrates the insusceptibility of intuitive knowing to conceptually based knowing than the act of falling in love. That love is a mode of intuitive knowing is evident, in the first place, from the fact that love amounts to the direct perception of and attraction to the beloved as a particular individual. In the second place, this perception of and attraction to the beloved as a particular individual is, for the lover, an intensely personal experience, in that it engages the lover not just mentally, but primarily emotively (via his deep-felt desire for the beloved), and volitionally (via his resolute intention to be united with the beloved.)

Bearing in mind that love is an eminently personal experience of the beloved *qua* individual, were someone to inquire as to why you love Susie, you might unwittingly attempt to oblige him in some such fashion as, "Well, she's beautiful, kind, intelligent, and has a wonderful sense of humor." Do these or like reasons effectively convey to the inquirer your experience of and attraction to Susie? Clearly, they do not, since such reasons amount to the (contradictory) attempt to justify your personal, and thus private, experience of Susie in an impersonal, and thus conceptually communicable, manner.

Still, so as to underscore further the futility of any would-be attempt to justify your love-experience, suppose the inquirer, upon hearing your recitation of Susie's attributes, were to remark, "You know, our mutual friend, Estelle, possesses qualities not unlike Susie's. Why then don't you love Estelle as much as Susie?" And what could you offer by way of response to this second query, save remarks to the effect that you love Susie more than Estelle because Susie "moves" you more than Estelle does. Which response, when you think about it, boils down to the blatantly circular assertion: "I love Susie because I love her (more than Estelle, notwithstanding that Estelle is possessed of qualities not unlike Susie's!")

But note: while I have been at pains to show how and why intuitive knowing is conceptually incommunicable, it would be a considerable mistake to conclude therefrom that intuitive knowing is absolutely incommunicable. As we have seen, if an event were *absolutely* incommunicable, it would be utterly beyond human understanding *and experience*. But intuitive knowing, whatever else it may be, is certainly an experience, albeit a very personal one. Hence, the possibility remains of communicating an intuitive experience *qua* experience. But how might one undertake to communicate a personal experience? The classic answer is by proposing experiences that may prove analogously meaningful to a particular individual.

As a case in point, let's recur to our aforementioned lover. Rather than resorting to conceptually based reasons in a vain attempt to explain to the inquirer why he loves Susie, such as her beauty, kindness, and intelligence, suppose that the lover takes the explanatory tack of comparing his love-experience to listening with rapt attention to a beautiful song, or losing oneself in the lush verdancy of nature, or the feeling of peace and joy one sometimes realizes when in the presence of true friends—or, if the inquirer has ever been in love himself, to the inquirer's own experience thereof. Of course, even if the lover does manage to convey his experience in this analogous manner, precisely because his experience is analogous, at once comparable and incomparable, he can never hope to convey the whole of his experience; it will ever remain an experience that, in the main, is *sui generis*, uniquely the lover's own.

Finally, if there is anything tantamount to objective evidence for intuitive experience, it is of a decidedly indirect kind, namely, the effect(s) such an experience has on the intuiter. And once again, let's take the intuition of love as illustrative of this point. Though personal and private, and thus largely incommunicable through normal conceptual channels, the experience of true love yet has a profoundly transformative effect on a person. Typically, the lover finds himself overflowing with peace, joy, a sense of personal well-being, a feeling of deep communion with and care for the beloved and, not infrequently, with other human and even non-human beings, as well. So that, while there is no direct evidential way of validating an intuitive experience, much less an intuitive experience of love, when we notice that a person's behavior has been significantly affected and even altered by his claimed experience—especially for the better—we have very good grounds for allowing that his claimed experience is an *actual* experience.

So much for what intuition is and how it differs from conceptual knowing. We are now better placed to appreciate why Lao Tzu maintains that conceptual knowing must be surpassed in favor of intuitive knowing, in favor of the "body's intelligence" (Poem 18), if our "minds [are to] be at one with the Tao." (Poem 21)

Clearly, Lao Tzu relates the decline of intuitive knowing to our "forgetfulness" of the Tao, and our recovery of intuitive knowing to our degree of reconnection with the Tao. As such, he implies that intuitive knowing can know the Tao in a way that far exceeds conceptual knowing. But what makes intuitive knowledge of the Tao superior to conceptual knowledge of the Tao? The answer is that intuitive knowing knows the Tao, not in the indirect, impersonal, and generalizing categorical manner of conceptual knowing, but rather in a direct, personal, and specific manner.

Which answer begets the further question: What does it mean to know the Tao in a direct, personal, and specific way? And here the answer is that intuitive knowledge of the Tao is, at bottom, a special mode of love-knowledge. For consider: if, as stated in earlier chapters, fear results from and is the sign of our illusory experience of dualism, and love issues from and is the sign of our non-illusory experience of union, then we must conclude that intuitive knowing, as direct, personal, and specific knowledge of the Tao, is thereby unified knowledge of the Tao, and so, at bottom, a special mode of love-knowledge.

The Reader has now detected my "ulterior motive" for illustrating intuitive knowing in the preceding paragraphs via the intuitive experience of love. Therein, I characterized love as a direct perception of and attraction to the beloved as a distinct individual. If so, then, insofar as one reunites with the Tao, and so, knows the Tao intuitively, one will have a direct perception of and attraction to the Tao as the Supreme and Unique Beloved. That the Tao is the Supreme and Unique Beloved is implicit from the discussion of the Tao's attributes in Chapter 1 (formlessness, perfection, infinity, unchangeability, eternity, and uniqueness) and Chapter 2 (Love Itself). To term the Tao the "Supreme and Unique Beloved" is but to encapsulate the point of these discussions of the Tao's attributes, since as all-perfect, infinite, unchangeable, and eternal Love Itself, the Tao is supremely and uniquely lovable, and therefore, the Supreme and Unique Object of Love. Whence my contention that to know the Tao intuitively is to experience the Tao as the Supreme and Unique Beloved.

Again, I stated in the above discussion of love that it is a profoundly personal experience, engaging the lover primarily emotively and volitionally (via his deeply felt desire for and determined intention to be united with the beloved), and only secondarily, mentally. For this reason, intuition of the Tao, as love-knowledge of the Tao, will be largely incommunicable conceptually, and only roughly communicable through experientially meaningful analogies. And because one's intuitive knowing of the Tao is a special mode of love-knowledge, a favorite analogous way (especially among mystics) of endeavoring to convey the flavor of one's intuitive grasp of the Tao is, not surprisingly, by appeal to the experience of human love—than which there is no better and more meaningful experience.

Yet again, I also stated that, while there is no direct, evidential way of communicating one's intuitive knowledge, there is yet an indirect evidential way to do so. As to love-knowledge as a mode of intuitive knowledge, this indirect method amounts to pointing to the positive effects such knowledge has on an individual, such as heightened peace and joy, and a deep sense of communion with and care for the beloved, as well as for other human and non-human beings. With specific reference to intuitive knowledge of the Tao as love-knowledge of the Tao, Lao Tzu highlights three positive effects that derive therefrom (see Chapter 4): greater inner "peace," a decrease in, if not elimination of, "sorrow" (physical and psychological suffering), and a dispelling of "confusion." What Lao Tzu understands by the first two of these positive effects—greater peace and a waning of sorrow—is fairly self-explanatory. What he has in mind when he suggests that a third positive effect of an intuitive grasp of the Tao is a release from confusion, probably warrants a few words of explanation.

In general, Lao Tzu's reference to "confusion" is synonymous with what in the parlance of the day may be termed "*un*enlightenment," as opposed, of course, to "enlightenment." But to suggest that a confused person is an unenlightened person clearly begs the question, since it presupposes understanding of what an enlightened person is. And it must be admitted that, concerning the defining features of enlightenment, there historically has been, and indeed continues to be, considerable debate. However, I believe that it is entirely in keeping with Lao Tzu's principles to suggest that by an enlightened person the great Sage intends an accelerated, albeit not perfect, capacity to "see," to "understand" reality as the Tao "sees" and "understands" reality.

Before all else, the transcendent, formless Tao views reality non-dualistically or interconnectedly. Accordingly, insofar as one is in touch with the Tao intuitively, one sees beyond the illusion of dualism and perceives reality interconnectedly. Moreover, to perceive reality interconnectedly is, as noted, a function of love; and love is itself ultimately a function of one's degree of union with the Tao. Hence, to perceive reality interconnectedly, as a function of one's degree of loving communion with the Tao, is to perceive reality lovingly. Last but not least, if to perceive reality interconnectedly is to perceive reality lovingly, then to the extent that one so perceives reality, one transcends love's dualistically begotten antithesis, fear—and in so doing, realizes greater peace and the waning of sorrow, in addition to the dissolution of confusion.

Then again, insofar as one cultivates one's intuitive connection to the Tao, one also begins *to see wisely*. That is, one develops one's capacity to apply knowledge appropriately in each concrete situation. Recall the foregoing depiction of intuition as a direct and immediate experience of, and insight into, a person, place, thing, or event. As such, intuitive knowing proceeds directly to the heart of an issue, without having to resort to conceptually based analysis, speculation, or inference. Intuitive knowing, in other words, simply knows what, how, and when to do, and not do, X in a given situation. Thus, an intuitively alert individual will be more prone to say the right thing to a person seeking her advice, more likely to make the right decision regarding a relationship, more apt to refrain from a course of action that will not be conducive to her or others' physical and/or psychological well-being, and so on.

But beyond even this benefit of intuitive knowing, insofar as such knowing is a direct result of one's loving communion with the Tao, the greater one's intuitive connection to the Tao, the greater will be one's capacity both to know and do the loving thing in a specific situation. Conversely, the less one's intuitive connection to the Tao, the less will be one's capacity to know and do the loving thing in a specific situation.[2]

Which brings us to yet another fundamental difficulty with law, morality, and religion, as far as Lao Tzu is concerned. Earlier, I noted that, as one loses sight of the Tao, and so abides in fear-based attachment, one experiences a diminution of one's naturally loving Nature. In light of the discussion of the nature and function of intuition, we must now add that one proportionally experiences a diminution of one's natural capacity *to know what is the loving thing to do in a given situation*. Accordingly, law, morality, and religion, as products of one's illusory separation from the Tao, entail, for Lao Tzu, the twofold simultaneous weakening of our natural capacity, not just to do the loving thing, but also to know what is the loving thing to do in a given situation.

However, should we transcend law, morality, and religion, that is, should "... powerful men and women ... remain centered in the Tao," and thereby recover their naturally loving Nature, "all things would be in harmony. The world would become a paradise. All people would be at peace, and the law"—legal, moral, and religious—"would be written in their hearts"—which is but to say, all people would be naturally loving *and* would spontaneously know what is the loving thing to do in a given situation. (See Poem 32)

Unfortunately, a world wherein the vast majority of "... men and women ... remain centered in the Tao ..." is an ideal yet to be realized. I say 'ideal yet to be realized' because, as noted in Chapter 4, Lao Tzu assures us that "Each separate being ... [will] return to the common source." (Poem 16) But until that wondrously harmonious and paradisal time, most people will fail to grasp that "the law"—legal, moral, and religious—"[is] ... written in their hearts." They will so fail because, not being centered in the Tao, their "... body's intelligence" (intuitive connection to the Tao) is in "decline." And with this large-scale "decline" in effect, people will be irresistibly drawn to law, morality, and religion for guidance, solace, courage, and inspiration. At precisely which point, Lao Tzu avers,

"Cleverness and knowledge step forth."

When one loses one's intuitive connection to the Tao, and, as a result, loses one's natural capacity to know and do the loving thing in a given situation, invariably, asserts Lao Tzu, one replaces intuitive knowing with "cleverness and knowledge." What does Lao Tzu mean by "cleverness and knowledge" as would-be substitutes for intuitive knowing?

Beginning with "cleverness," while there is certainly room for disagreement as to Lao Tzu's intended meaning here, I submit that by cleverness in the present context, the Sage primarily intends the fostering of mental acuity in the realization of one's goals. Or, to state the point somewhat more bluntly, we might say that cleverness in Lao Tzu's sense of the term refers, in the main, to the development of one's mental capacity in the service of getting what one wants.

Now, in principle, there is certainly nothing wrong with developing a mentally nimble capacity to realize one's goals and aspirations. We all need to develop the ability to adroitly apply means to ends, if we are to realize not just such material goals as wealth, power, success, and status, but even such exalted spiritual goals as selfless love and union with the Source. Indeed, far too many individuals either aren't sure what they want, or else know what they want but are at a loss as to how to achieve what they want. And in this world at least, not to know how to realize one's goals, and worse yet, not even to have goals to realize, is to fail of self-actualization, spiritually as well as materially.

Well, if cleverness, in the sense of applying suitable means to the achievement of a desired goal, is evidently indispensable to the realization of a fulfilled life both materially and spiritually, why would Lao Tzu see fit to assert that cleverness is but a third-rate substitute for intuitive knowing? Principally, I suggest, because cleverness that is born of one's disconnection from the Tao will be cleverness largely unsuffused with love, and thus largely suffused with fear. It will, in short, be a fear-based or attached cleverness. Clever folks ridden with fear, and thus with little or no sense of communion with others, will pursue their goals with little or no concern for others' feelings and well-being. They will find it all too easy to resort to manipulation and generally to use others to gain their ends. Even worse, fear-beset clever ones, regarding others as dangerous, will be more liable to view others as threats to the realization of their goals, and so, will be more apt to resort to physical and psychological acts of violence in quest of their goals.

But doubtless worst of all, will be those clever ones who pursue their ends prompted by moral, religious, or legal zeal. As noted earlier, Lao Tzu points to such individuals when he writes:

> The moral man does something.
> and when no one responds
> he rolls up his sleeves and uses force. (Poem 38)

Such individuals, unimbued with love, are notorious for pursuing their ends with a ferocity, tenacity, and ruthlessness inspired by the usually unshakeable conviction that theirs is a morally, religiously, or legally ordained course of action, and therefore, a morally, religiously, or legally righteous course of action. Unmotivated by love, all too often morally , religiously , or legally driven clever ones succumb to zealotry, from which it is but a short step to the virtually nihilistic position that, in quest of their morally, religiously, or legally just and prescribed ends, "just about anything goes!" After all, are not abortion clinics clearly and flagrantly in violation of traditional morality and the law of God? Well, then, let's destroy them and, for good measure, assassinate their medical staff. Are not gays and lesbians patently at odds with the Bible, traditional morality, and in some states at least, the law? Well, then, let's feel free to abuse them physically and psychologically, even to the extent of invoking the wrath of God upon them. Are not those who insult, whether consciously or unconsciously, our religion's God committing, as the various Holy Books attest, a heinous sin? Well, then, let's violently retaliate against these infidels in the name of our God. Are not those who disobey the law culpable, despite the circumstances surrounding their actions, in light of the long-standing principle: "Ignorance of the law is no excuse?" Well, then, let's prosecute these violators to the full extent of the law, and clemency be damned! And so it acrimoniously goes for all-too many a moral, religious, or legal clever one unimbued with the unified consciousness born of love.[3]

And no less, insists Lao Tzu, does "knowledge step forth" when, and to the extent that, one's intuitive connection to the Tao is weakened. One's intuitive connection to the Tao, recall, enables one to apply knowledge appropriately, and most importantly, lovingly, in a specific situation. This ability to so apply knowledge is what one loses when, and to the extent that, one's intuitive connection to the Tao is severed, and in two principal ways.

In the first place, let's assume that someone is absolutely convinced as to the rightness of a certain moral, religious, or legal principle. Let's say, for example, that a person is committed to the moral prescription to act justly, the religious command to honor one's father and mother, and the sacredness of the rule of law. Even granting the objective and absolute status of these principles, that is, even allowing that these principles must be obeyed without exception and despite one's personal feelings, beliefs, and prejudices, the more complicated the situation, the more difficult it becomes to know how to apply such universally binding moral, religious, and legal principles in a given, concrete situation. In which difficult-to-apply regard, consider two illustrative cases in point:

Case 1: A man is on the verge of death, but you and his doctor are the only ones privy to this information. You also know that this man has a deep-seated and unrelenting fear of death. What is the moral, the just thing to do in this situation? Do you owe it to this man to tell him as soon as you can, to delay telling him, or even to avoid telling him that his demise is imminent? If you yourself aren't inclined to apprise this man of such painful news, do you leave it to his doctor to break the news, or else inform his relatives and/or close friends and abandon the decision to them? Then too, suppose you do decide that the morally just thing to do is to tell this man that he is dying. How do you go about telling him? Do you simply blurt it out and let the chips fall where they may, or wait for the right moment to tell him? And if the latter, how do you adjudge that the right moment is indeed the right moment? In short, even knowing/believing that you are duty-bound to act justly in a given situation is in itself no guarantee that you will know what is the just course of action in a given situation.

Case 2: Your parents own a profitable business and have groomed you for years to succeed them therein. For your part, you had every intention of taking charge of the business after your parents retired, and in fact, eagerly looked forward to the challenge. Now at age twenty-five, you experience a sudden change of heart: Your once ardent desire to assume the reins of your parents' business has mysteriously vanished. What you now strongly desire is to attend college, attain a degree in education, and become an elementary school teacher. Being a religious person, you believe strongly in the Ten Commandments, not the least of which is the fifth: "Honor thy father and mother." What is the honorable thing to do in this situation? In an effort to resolve this dilemma, you reflect as follows. "My parents have been priming me and counting on me to be their successor for twenty-five years. And I've given them absolutely no reason to doubt the sincerity of my desire to follow in their business footsteps. I well know that should I now decide not to succeed them, this would not only devastate them, but they would certainly, and doubtless angrily, shut down a business into which for over fifty years they poured their hearts and souls. And yet, I know that what I really want to do with my life—at least, as far as I can now determine—is teach, and that to delay pursuing this goal, say, until my parents' death, in order to head up their business would be extremely difficult for me. What, in view of all these considerations, is the honorable thing to do, as far as my father and mother are concerned?"

The above cases illustrate the difficulty one often has when attempting to apply one's firm moral and religious principles in concrete situations, when and to the extent that one loses one's intuitive connection to the Tao. (Which is perhaps what Lao Tzu has in mind when he writes: "The kind man does something, yet something remains undone. The just man does something, and leaves many things to be done." [Poem 38])

But there is a second and even less fruitful way that "... knowledge steps forth" when and to the extent that one's intuitive communion with the Tao is lost. I allude to the fact that far too many, not only find it difficult to apply moral, religious, and legal principles in concrete situations; they frequently find it difficult, if not impossible, to determine *which* moral view, religious tradition, or code of law is the "true" moral view, religious tradition, or code of law. Worse yet, when they survey the multiplicity and diversity of competing and often contradictory moralities, religions, and legal systems, some either throw up their hands in despair at ever settling on a true morality, religion, or legal system, or else conclude that there is no true morality, religion, and legal system, and hence that the quest for truth itself is but a vain and meaningless enterprise. And with this despairing of truth, we come to what is doubtless a "worst case scenario" when "knowledge steps forth" to fill the void left by one's diminished intuitive communion with the Tao.

For all these reasons, then, Lao Tzu finds morality, religion, and law sorely wanting as antidotes to the sorrow, confusion, and dearth of inner peace that afflict humankind. There is only one way to overcome this threefold affliction, he assures us, and that is by recovering one's true, loving Nature, and thereby, both the power to do the loving thing and the intuitive capacity to know what is the loving thing to do in each specific situation. But ...

Does this Mean that Lao Tzu Advocates the *Absolute* Rejection of Morality, Religion, and Law?

He does not, and in support thereof, consider, first, the following passages:

> If a country is governed with tolerance,
> the people are comfortable and honest.
> If a country is governed with repression,
> the people are depressed and crafty. (Poem 58)
>
> Governing a large country
> is like frying a small fish.
> You spoil it with too much poking.
> Center your country in the Tao
> and evil will have no power. (Poem 60)
>
> If you want to learn how to govern,
> avoid being clever or rich.
> The simplest pattern is the clearest.
> Content with an ordinary life,
> you can show all people the way
> back to their own true nature. (Poem 65)

As these passages amply attest, Lao Tzu not only speaks explicitly of governing a country, he also puts forth views on: (1)the characteristics of good governing (namely, tolerance, temperance, simplicity, and, above all, being centered in the Tao), (2) the characteristics of bad governing (namely, repression, excessive intrusiveness, cleverness, and the lure of wealth), (3) the consequences of bad governing (namely, fostering a depressed and crafty citizenry, and generally perpetuating evil in the land), and (4) the ultimate purpose of governing (namely, to "show all people the way back to their own true nature.")

Now, as a primary component of governing is legislation, it is clear that Lao Tzu cannot but own the necessity of laws. And though he fails to speak in a like explicit fashion concerning the necessity of moral and religious principles, in light of his acceptance of laws, as well as his tendency to lump morality, religion, and law together as the main would-be surrogates for a direct communion with the Tao, there is no reason to doubt that the Sage is equally prepared to own the necessity of moral and religious principles.

But how can Lao Tzu regard morality, religion, and law as necessities, if they are, as he believes, egregiously inadequate substitutes for a direct communion with the Tao? The answer is that he regards them as necessities *as things now stand*, and the way things now stand is that, as is all-too evident, the vast majority of the human race have yet to realize a direct communion with the Tao, and so, have yet to realize fully their naturally loving Nature

In view of this unrealized, less-than-fully loving present human condition, we may infer from Lao Tzu's heretofore-discussed views on morality, religion, and law that he regards them as serving three main *provisional* purposes. For one thing, given most of humankind's illusory separation from the Tao, and the consequent attachment-born condition of sorrow, confusion, and lack of inner peace that plague them, morality, religion, and law serve, however imperfectly, as temporary sources of comfort and hope against this threefold human, all-too human condition. For another thing, given that most human beings have yet to be in full possession of their naturally loving Nature, and so, are more apt to commit, in thought and word, as well as in deed, fear-based acts of violence against one another, morality, religion, and law serve, however imperfectly and temporarily, to temper and restrain somewhat man's inhumanity to man, in particular, and to everything else, in general. And finally, given that human beings' natural capacity to act lovingly has been diminished, resulting in a waning of faith in their inherent goodness, wholeness, and aptitude, morality, religion, and law serve, however imperfectly, as temporary sources of guidance and purpose when, and to the extent that, human beings"... no longer trust themselves." (Poem 72)

Such, then, are the primary services morality, religion, and law render a "fallen" humanity. However, as these "servants" are themselves human inventions, products of humanity's "forgetfulness" of its true, loving Nature, they will ever prove hopelessly inadequate as solutions to the sorrow, confusion, and lack of inner peace that are humanity's threefold, overriding scourge. The only real and lasting solution to this tripart malady, Lao Tzu insists, rests in finding one's way back to one's true, loving Nature. For Lao Tzu's general prescription for returning to one's "Primal Self" (Poem 28), I give you Chapter 6.

Notes

1. I would note that the *Tao Te Ching* is not alone in its contention that morality, religion, and law must be surpassed in the interest of true spiritual advancement. We find this same theme played out in Hinduism, in its view that morality and ethics *(dharma)*, and by implication, religion and law, represent only the third stage of spiritual evolution, a stage that must give way to the fourth and final stage, that of *moksha* or liberation. In Buddhism, we note that the Buddha's third and most insidious temptation is an ethical one, a great stream of "shoulds" by which Mara (popular Buddhism's Satan) attempted to instill fear in the Buddha and thereby jar him out of his state of unified, non-dual consciousness. In the West, the father of Christian Existentialism, Søren Kierkegaard (1813–1855), in his "stages of life" presents a partial version of this transcending motif. Kierkegaard holds that, if one is to do full justice to one's uniqueness as an individual, one must move beyond the guidance afforded by the ethical stage, and make a "leap of faith," by which one enters the Religious Stage, wherein one establishes a personal relationship with Christ, Who alone can do full justice to one's individuality. According to Kierkegaard, then, religion, in the sense of a personal relationship with Christ, constitutes the pinnacle of spiritual success. Despite this notable difference from the *Tao Te Ching*, however, remove the Christian assumptions underlying Kierkegaard's views, primarily that we must establish a personal relationship with Christ, and there are interesting parallels between his and Lao Tzu's position that our goal is to realize an intuitive, and thus

personal, communion with the Tao. Finally, the view that one must transcend morality, religion, and law is thoroughly in line with both Eastern and Western mysticism, for which realizing personal communion with the Source is the consummate goal of existence and the crowning achievement of spirituality.

2. In Chapter 4, I suggested that confusion denotes such negative mental states as error, ignorance, misunderstanding, doubt, delusion, misguided and/or failed aspirations and goals. Such mental states we may regard as symptomatic of the unenlightened individual. In this chapter, I endeavor to specify those states of mind symptomatic of the non-confused or enlightened individual, to wit, the spiritual Master.

3. Concerning acts of violence, which moral, religious, and legal zealotry tends to condone, Lao Tzu has this to say: “”For every force there is a counterforce. Violence, even well intentioned, always rebounds upon oneself.” (Poem 30)

CHAPTER SIX

Recovering Our True Self: Hints from Nature

Be like the forces of nature . . .
LAO TZU, *Tao Te Ching*, POEM 23

Recovering Our True Self: The Way of Meditation

Before proceeding to examine Lao Tzu's "natural" approach to spirituality, in general, and recovering our true,Tao-Nature, in particular, it is interesting to note that he was well aware of, and indeed plainly endorsed, a more traditional approach to said recovery, namely, what I shall style "the way of sitting meditation." Two passages from the *Tao Te Ching* are especially revelatory in this meditative regard:

> Close your mouth,
> block off your senses,
> blunt your sharpness,
> untie your knots,
> soften your glare,
> settle your dust:
> This is the primal identity. (Poem 56)

> Without opening your door,
> you can open your heart to the world.
> Without looking out your window,
> you can see the essence of the Tao. (Poem 47)

The former passage clearly depicts a person engaged in sitting meditation: a comfortable location, relaxed body, senses under control, eyes either half-closed or completely closed, and concludes by equating the meditative process with "the primal identity," our true, loving Nature. The latter passage, which more obliquely suggests sitting meditation, emphasizes, however metaphorically, that such meditation is a way to "see the essence of the Tao," that is, to realize an intuitive connection to and insight into the Tao (see Chapter 5).

But precisely what is it about mediation, whether sitting or otherwise, as we shall see, that makes it a prime and time-honored method of recovering our "primal identity" and "seeing the essence of the Tao"? The answer is linked to the essence of meditation, to what meditation essentially is. And what meditation essentially amounts to is *undistracted focus for a positive purpose*. Thus, any activity that fosters undistracted focus for a positive purpose counts as meditation. Meditative practices run the gamut from such traditional sitting-meditative forms as repeating a mantra or concentrating on either an inner or external image, to such seemingly mundane activities as walking, running, exercising, swimming, ironing!, doing dishes!, dancing, cooking, and so on. Ultimately, the meditative ideal is to make one's very life a meditation: to bring one's full and undivided attention to whatever one is doing; to be, like the focused athlete, continuously "in the [life] zone."

Unfortunately, the situation focus-wise for most individuals is far from the meditative ideal. In fact, the concentrative condition of most individuals might well be characterized as one of varying degrees of *distracted unfocus*. Zen Buddhism (a spirituality derived primarily from Taoism and Mahayana Buddhism, by the way) alludes to the largely non-focused status of most individuals with such koanic utterances as, "When you eat, you do not eat," "When you play, you do not play."

The point of these and like cryptic remarks is that most individuals' daily doings, especially those that are important to them, are fraught with mainly fear-based distractions concerning the past, present, and future. That is, most individuals, when, say, they're eating, are not simply eating (in a focused manner), but are, whether consciously or no, more or less distracted by issues and concerns relating to the past (e.g., "Why didn't the boss comment on my report yesterday?"), the present (e.g., "Does the fetching lady to whom I'm talking find me attractive?"), and the future (e.g., "Am I ever going to achieve financial independence?") In light of our discussion in Chapter 5, wherein we learned that fear is the dour distinguishing feature of attachment, we might also characterize the concentrative condition of most individuals as one of greater or lesser attachment concerning past, present, and future outcomes.

In Chapter 5 we further noticed that the attached state takes its toll on an individual physically and psychologically, as well as spiritually. Insofar as attachment impedes one's ability to focus undistractedly, it is apparent that one of the principal ways in which attachment disadvantages an individual physically and psychologically is by scattering said individual's energies to the proverbial four winds. In other words, the attachment-beset individual not only experiences a drain on his energy; he will also be incapable of giving himself fully and undividedly to any person, situation, activity, or project, and as a result, will be incapable of realizing his full potential physically and psychologically.

Still, if the price one pays physically and psychologically as a result of one's attachment-born distracted state is bad enough, even worse is the related spiritual price one pays when, and to the extent that, one lives a distracted life. To appreciate the spiritual price one pays herein requires that we delve more deeply into the essence of meditation. Recall that the essence of meditation consists of a state of undistracted focus for a positive purpose, such that one is no longer bedeviled by especially fear-based distractions pertaining to the past, present, and future. If this is what meditation essentially entails, this must mean that to truly meditate is actually to abide in the Now or the Moment.

The Now or the Moment we may define as a temporal point, or, if you prefer, a state of supra-temporality, meaning that the Now/Moment transcends the temporal divisions of past, present, and future. But the transcendence of time is, as we've seen, the definition of the eternal. And the eternal, we further saw, is an attribute of the transcendent Tao. Accordingly, to meditate, and thereby to transcend time by dint of being in the Now/Moment, is to experience the Eternal ("see the essence of the Tao"), and thus to commune with the Tao Itself!

Depending on how advanced a meditator is, his time-transcending communion with the Tao may span but a few seconds or persist for several hours, temporally speaking.* Still, however "long" one remains in the meditative state, such communion with the "eternal Tao" cannot but redound greatly to the meditator's spiritual benefit. And this because communion with the Tao, as Chapter 5 showed, is an intuitive experience of love with the Tao That is Love. For this reason, the meditator will, on the one hand, realize greater freedom from the main effects of a dualistic consciousness, namely, fear (attachment), confusion, sorrow, and a lack of inner peace, and, on the other hand, realize more fully the main effects of a unified consciousness, namely, fearlessness (non-attachment), knowing the loving thing to do (non-confusion), physical and psychological well-being (non-sorrow), and greater inner peace.

In an even more profound sense, however, the true meditator, insofar as he reconnects with the "eternal Tao," reconnects with his true, loving Tao-Nature. For, as I noted in Chapter 2, when the Tao creates It creates in and from Its Own infinite Being. Which implies that when the Tao creates, It literally creates Itself in and through Its manifold of forms. In short, our "Primal Identity" (Poem 56), our "True Nature" (Poem 65) is nothing less than an immanent expression of the Tao. And since, moreover, the Tao is Love, our True Nature,

---

* If the juxtaposing of "time-transcendence" with "temporally speaking" strikes you as contradictory, bear in mind that "temporally speaking" refers to our physical, embodied condition, "time-transcendence" to our focused consciousness in the meditative state.

as an immanent expression of the Tao, cannot but be naturally loving. Whence, meditatively to commune with the Tao is to recover, to reconnect with, even if but briefly, our true, loving Tao-Nature.

Above, I said that the meditative ideal is to make one's life a meditation, to reach a point where living in the Now/Moment becomes habitual. Such an ideal, of course, requires considerable practice and perseverance in a specific form of meditation, such as sitting meditation. As one perseveringly practices a meditative form, one gradually acquires the ability to apply the focused meditative state, the state of being in the Now/Moment, to more and more areas of one's day-to-day life—until, imperceptibly but inevitably, as I say, one's very life becomes a meditation. (At which point, I would parenthetically note, the meditator fulfills Jesus's injunction "to pray continually" [Luke 18: 1, The Jerusalem Bible]. For what, in the final analysis, is prayer but communion with God/the Tao. And as the meditator whose life is a meditation abides in a state of continuous communion with God/the Tao, his life at the same time becomes a life of sustained prayerful communion with God/the Tao.)

Recovering Our True Self: Hints from Nature

If Lao Tzu is foursquare in agreement with virtually all spiritual teachers who subscribe to meditation as an indispensable means of reconnecting with the Tao, and thereby, of recovering our True Nature, our "Primal Identity"—even if these teachers may not always agree with Lao Tzu's contention that this Nature is a divine Self-expression of the Tao (see Chapter 2)—the great Sage is equally convinced that if we attend to nature writ large, if, that is, we carefully attend to the way the natural world operates, we will discern a way of life perhaps even more effective than that of meditation whereby we can recover our true, Tao-Nature. The guiding idea here is that the natural order is the purest, the most "natural" expression of the *immanent* Tao. In which case, to study the forces of nature, and then to "be like the forces of nature" (Poem 23), is to be like the Tao Itself, and thus to live in a way perfectly suited to recovering our true, Tao-Nature.

In the balance of this chapter I shall list, and then comment upon, salient passages from the *Tao Te Ching* that refer to various, seemingly random lessons of nature concerning the Tao, ourselves, and how we might recover our True Nature. Afterwards, in Chapters 7 and 8, I shall suggest that all such nature-inspired lessons finally resolve to two integrally related *fundamental* lessons, namely, the lesson of letting go (Chapter 7), and the lesson of acceptance of self, of others, and of the world (Chapter 8).

~

To begin our survey of "nature-passages" in the *Tao Te Ching*, consider the following:

> The supreme good is like water,
> which nourishes all things without trying to.
> It is content with the low places that people disdain.
> Thus it is like the Tao. (Poem 8)

Water, a favorite metaphor in Lao Tzu's spirituality, is here likened to the "supreme good," and thus to the Tao, which of course *is* the Supreme Good. Water teaches us about the Tao in many symbolic ways, not the least of which is that, like the Tao, water is the prime source of nourishment, and so of life itself. Indeed, over two-thirds of the body's weight consists of water, and seemingly solid muscle mass comprises more than 90 percent water. In light of the preponderance of water in organisms' physical makeup, we may well say that, in a sense, an organism *is* water in the guise of form, just as we may say that all created things *are* the Tao Self-expressing Itself formally in and though them.

Again, water "nourishes all things without trying to." By being true to its own nature, its own natural course, water nourishes all things. In a similar manner, the Tao, and by extension, each of the Tao's Self-manifestations, especially Its *human* Self-manifestations, "nourishes and completes all things" (Poem 41) by being true to Its own specific nature,* and especially, by living in accord with its own *naturally loving* nature (a point elaborated on in the concluding chapter.)

Yet again, "water is content with the low places that people disdain." Water, whose flow naturally seeks the low ground, mirrors the Tao's humility, and in two principal ways. For one thing, the Tao is content to remain "hidden" to most, even though, as infinite Reality, It is "always present" to them (Poem 4). For another, since the immanent Tao, the Tao that "is merged with all things," is content to remain "hidden in people's hearts, it can [also] be called humble." (Poem 34)

The lesson for us is clear: if the infinite and all-powerful Tao sees fit to humble Itself, then we too should see fit to humble ourselves. But then, what exactly does it mean to humble oneself? Typically, a humble person is thought of as someone who is not arrogant, not vain, not pretentious, and so on. Such characterizations, while certainly true indicators of humility, are still only negative indicators; they tell us what it means not to be humble, not what it means to be humble.

So, in the interest of a more positive characterization of humility, let's pose the question this way: What is it that humility *essentially* consists of? And that would essentially be, I submit, a truthful assessment of one's personal qualities, good as well as not so good! Indeed—and here is an aspect of humility that often goes unnoticed—it is no less a mark of *non*-humility to fail to appreciate or, worse yet, to deny one's good qualities than it is to overlook or deny one's negative qualities. Or, to state the latter point in more affirmative terms, if the defining feature of humility is in fact truthfulness with and about oneself, it is no less an act of humility to own one's good character traits, talents, good deeds, etc., than it is to own one's negative character traits, lack of talent, bad deeds, etc. In either case, to fail of humility is to fail to

* By "specific nature" I mean each individual's unique personality, namely, the ensemble of environmental influences, temperament, mental, emotional, and physical traits, personal maturity and spiritual evolvement, that continuously interact to forge our shared human/divine Nature into *this* human/divine being.

take the first step to physical, psychological, and spiritual wholeness, a point developed by other *Tao Te Ching* passages, as shortly we shall see.

Moreover, it goes without saying that humility is particularly appropriate for those who aspire to be leaders.

> If you want to govern the people,
> you must place yourself below them.
> If you want to lead the people,
> you must learn how to follow them. (Poem 66)

And,

> The best leader
> follows the will of the people. (Poem 68)

Both passages echo the New Testament's "The last shall be first" (Mark 10:31) principle. The true leader doesn't lord it over others, but, on the contrary, regards herself as the servant of others. ("If you want to govern the people, you must place yourself below them.") Indeed, the ideal leader leads in such a way that,

> When his work is done,
> the people say, "Amazing:
> we did it, all by ourselves!" (Poem 17)

In this same vein, the true leader is attuned to the people she leads, is someone, that is, who, while never compromising the truth as she knows it, takes her cue from and tailors her guidance to the needs, mentality, tastes, and mood of the people in question. ("If you want to lead the people, you must learn how to follow them," you must learn, that is, to "follow the will of the people.")

Such attunement to and readiness to serve the people also requires of the leader an extraordinary degree of humility for two related reasons. First, to be a true leader one must be prepared to undergo an intense and probably protracted self-scrutiny of his attachment-begotten faults and failings, as the requisite prior condition of overcoming them, a scrutiny Lao Tzu undoubtedly has in mind when he notes that,

> When a great man makes a mistake, he realizes it.
> Having realized it, he admits it.
> Having admitted it, he corrects it.
> He considers those who point out his faults
> as his most benevolent teachers. (Poem 61)

Finally, the leader who is the servant of and in tune with the people must needs be a highly detached person. For only such a person can so love the people as to serve them without expecting anything in return (see Poem 51) *and* has cultivated the intuitive sensitivity and insight required to conform herself to the people's needs, mentality, tastes, and mood.[1]

Recurring to the lessons water has to teach us about recovering our true, Tao-Nature, consider the following paradoxical stanza:

> Nothing in the world
> is as soft and yielding as water.
> Yet for dissolving the hard and inflexible,
> nothing can surpass it. (Poem 78)

Here, the activity of water suggests the Tao's infinitely loving Nature, the truth that the Tao is "Love Itself" (see Chapter 2). Just as water is the most "soft and yielding" of substances in the world, so the Tao, as Love Itself, is the most caring and detached of realities (see Poem 51). Yet, though "Nothing... is as soft and yielding as water," it is unsurpassed in its ability to "dissolve the hard and inflexible." Water is unsurpassed herein because it is, so to speak, the most patient and persevering of substances. In this respect, water also reflects the infinite patience and perseverance of the Tao, Which well knows that "Whoever is born stiff and inflexible is a disciple of death" (that is, a practitioner of attachment, and so of a life lived in disconnection from the Tao that is Life), whereas "Whoever is soft and yielding is a disciple of life" (that is, a devotee of detachment, and so of a life lived in union with the Tao that is Life. [Poem 76]) Ultimately, we may rest assured that just as water inevitably and inexorably "dissolves the hard and the inflexible," so, thanks to the Tao's infinite patience and persistence,

> The hard and the stiff will be broken.
> The soft and the supple will prevail. (Poem 76)

Which is only to say that the *really* good news of the *Tao Te Ching* is that,

> All things end in the Tao
> as rivers flow into the sea. (Poem 32)

In a final "watery" passage, patience is again highlighted, but this time with specific reference to our trusting in the Tao, particularly when the sorrows and confusions of life are "too much with us." The passage reads:

> Do you have the patience to wait
> till your mud settles and the water is clear?
> Can you remain unmoving
> till the right action arises by itself? (Poem 15)

Muddy water, we know, clears most readily when left unperturbed. Impatiently agitating water only prolongs its muddy condition. The best and most expedient course of action, accordingly, if it is clear water that we're after, is non-action, to bear ourselves in patience "till the right action arises by itself," till, that is, nature takes its natural cleansing course.

Once again, the lesson for us is clear: the infinitely patient and constant Tao will in due course clear up our attachment-born physical, mental, and emotional "mud," if we, like the Tao, can remain patiently "unmoving till the right action arises by itself."

But precisely what is Lao Tzu suggesting here? Is he telling us that patience in the sense of sheer passivity is the optimal way to move beyond our attachment-begotten struggles? In other words, Is he preaching a doctrine of literal non-action as the most effective way of dealing with our problems and generally of comporting ourselves in our day-to-day lives?

When we review the many passages in the *Tao Te Ching* calling for "non-action," we may be tempted to conclude that a doctrine of literal non-action is indeed what Lao Tzu is advocating as the proper course of action for those in tune with the Tao! Thus, he writes:

> The Tao never does anything,
> yet through it all things are done. (Poem 37)

> Practice not-doing,
> and everything will fall into place. (Poem 3)

> The gentlest thing in the world
> overcomes the hardest thing in the world.
> That which has no substance
> enters where there is no space.
> This shows the value of non-action.
> Teaching without words,
> performing without actions:
> that is the Master's way. (Poem 43)[2]

As these passages indicate, non-action is the way of the Tao Itself, and so, (1) the way in which "everything will fall into place," (2) the way of the true Master, and (3) the way of the natural order, which, as the purest expression of the Tao, most perfectly "shows the value of non-action."

Granting, then, that "non-action" is the way of the Tao, let us ask anew the question: Is Lao Tzu actually suggesting that the wisest and most expedient way to overcome life's sorrows and confusions, and generally to live our lives, is to live a life of sheer non-action? The answer must be a resounding no! For, in the first place, I think all would agree that Lao Tzu, in advocating non-action, can't be advocating a life of *literal* non-action, since to advocate same is to advocate a blatant contradiction. Moreover, the "gentlest thing in the world" is certainly doing something as it works to "overcome the hardest thing in the world," an activity Lao Tzu styles "non-action."[3] Evidently, then, when the Sage speaks of "non-action," he doesn't intend thereby absolute non-action but rather a *certain kind of action*.

The following citations provide an initial glimpse at the kind of action Lao Tzu envisions when he speaks of "non-action":

> The Master doesn't think about his actions;
> they flow from the core of his being. (Poem 50)

> Act without doing;
> work without effort. (Poem 63)

> The Master takes action
> by letting things take their course.
> He remains as calm
> at the end as at the beginning. (Poem 64)

From these citations we may gather that, by non-action, Lao Tzu understands a kind of action that is at once spontaneous (Poem 50), effortless (Poem 63), peaceful and that "lets things take their [natural] course." (Poem 64). Were we to epitomize these four defining features of "non-action" in a single phrase, may I suggest that collectively they resolve to "detached action"? And this because each defining feature of "non-action" assumes, in its way, the transcending of attachment, and thus, in its way, the realization of detachment, and does so as follows.

In the first place, if attachment entails the dualistic illusion that one exists in separation from the Tao, in particular, and all else, in general, then the attached state correspondingly entails a weakening, and the detached state a strengthening, of one's intuitive connection to the Tao, as we saw in Chapter 5. But intuition is the cognitive source of spontaneous action, in that intuition transcends conceptual, inferential, and deliberative—in a word, non-spontaneous—knowing, and effects a direct and immediate—in a word, spontaneous—insight into a person, place, thing, or event, and ultimately, into the Tao Itself, thereby facilitating spontaneous action. So that, if spontaneous action is a function of intuition, and intuition rests on detachment, which in its turn is a result of reconnecting especially with the Tao, then spontaneous action, as a defining feature of "non-action," is a mode of "detached action."

In the second place, if to be attached insures that one's life will be more or less assailed by humankind's three chief afflictions, confusion, sorrow, and a dearth of inner peace, then the attached life is plainly at odds with an effortless life, and an effortless life is just as plainly in keeping with a detached life.[4] Whence, my contention that effortlessness, as a defining feature of "non-action," is a second mode of "detached action."

In the third place, if an attached life begets a life of non-spontaneity and ongoing effort, as we've just seen, then an attached life is evidently entirely incompatible with a life wherein one "lets things take their course," whereas a detached life is just as evidently completely compatible with such a life. Therefore, my contention that a life in tune with the natural flow of things, as a defining feature of "non-action," is a third mode of "detached action."

Finally, if inner peace is an infallible sign of love, and so of one's connection to the Tao that *is* Love (see Chapter 4), then the attached life, which issues from belief in one's separation from the Tao, is entirely inconsistent with a life infused with inner peace, whereas a life of inner peace is entirely consistent with a life of detachment. Thus, my contention that inner peace, as a defining feature of "non-action," is a fourth mode of "detached action."

For these reasons, I submit that by "non-action" in the *Tao Te Ching* Lao Tzu fundamentally intends "detached action." Still, if "detached action" is what Lao Tzu intends by "non-action" herein, then clearly he understands thereby an *ideal sort of action*. He implies as much by repeatedly stating that "non-action" is action solely befitting the "Master," the spiritually enlightened one. But beyond any such implication as to the ideal status of "non-action," if such action is in fact all one with "detached action," then such action necessarily presupposes and issues from a profound degree of communion with the Tao, as evidenced most conspicuously by the Master's intuitive spontaneity, effortless life, readiness to let things take their natural course, and imperturbable inner peace. In other words, "detached action" is an unfailing sign that one has realized the goal, indeed, the very culmination, of spirituality: loving communion with the Tao That is Love.* Suffice it to say that herein lies nature's foremost *promissory* message.

Even so, there remains the ever-so practical task of getting to this final "Promised Land" of spiritual perfection. To which practical end, Lao Tzu, surveying further the natural order, counsels us to

> Be like the forces of nature:
> when it blows, there is only wind;
> when it rains, there is only rain;
> when the clouds pass, the sun shines through.
> (Poem 23)

To "Be like the forces of nature" we must be humble, we must, that is, be honest with ourselves and others. Nature neither makes excuses

---

*The practice of "non-action" is a consequence of *Te* (see Introduction), the experience of true Tao-Power, manifested, most notably, by action marked by intuitive spontaneity, effortlessness, relinquishing control, and unfailing inner peace. In other words, "non-action" as a consequence of *Te*, is a surefire sign that one has realized the ideal, the ultimate goal of spirituality, loving communion with the Tao That is Love.

for nor denies its present condition ("when it rains, there is only rain"). For example, if we're angry, or addicted, or confused, or physically out of sorts, Lao Tzu would have us forthrightly acknowledge these unpleasant physical, mental, and emotional conditions. And why? Because, as nature further indicates, such forthrightness is the most expedient way to move beyond these difficult conditions ("when the clouds pass, the sun shines through.")

Nature's call to personal honesty is also the theme of the following poem, the first stanza of which reads:

> If you want to shrink something,
> you must first allow it to expand.
> If you want to get rid of something,
> you must first allow it to flourish.
> If you want to take something,
> you must first allow it to be given.
> This is called the subtle perception
> of the way things are. (Poem 36)

If we are in touch with "the way things are," we will observe that the first step in healing a physical, mental, or emotional disorder is, as Poem 23 suggests, honestly to admit the fact of our disorder. But along with this message Poem 36 adds the insight that ridding ourselves of a disorder typically involves a period wherein a person goes to extremes with respect to that disorder. ("If you want to shrink something, you must first allow it to expand"). For example, say the disorder in question is a fear of self-expression. In this case, overcoming this fear, especially if it has been a long-standing one, will almost certainly require an intervening period wherein the person's behavior is largely dominated by extremes of self-assertiveness resulting from extremes of anger and impatience.

Nor is it difficult to fathom the why of such extreme behavior. After all, a person long habituated to not expressing herself can hardly be expected immediately to reverse this habitual fear-based trend. An ingrained behavioral disposition, which of course is what a habit is, requires time and effort to unlearn and relearn especially an opposite behavioral disposition. In the meantime, a person, unpracticed in a mode of behavior, such as that of positive self-expression, having little or no previous experience to draw on, can only test the behavioral waters, so to speak, by experimenting in a largely trial-and-error manner with behaviors that, in this case, more or less approximate acts of positive self-expression.

Moreover, because a person habituated to non-self-expression will doubtless harbor a sizable amount of residual anger and frustration at having for so long repressed herself, her initial efforts at positive self-expression, as above was noted, will usually elicit compensatory extremes of self-assertiveness in the form of extremes of anger and impatience. Her anger will be in proportion to the *degree* of her non-self-expression; her impatience in proportion to the *length* of her non-self-expression. Eventually, as she comes to own and accept her anger and impatience herein, these extreme emotive responses will give way to their opposites, greater peace and patience, resulting in more positive and balanced acts of self-expression. Which movement from unbalanced to balanced behavior the *Tao Te Ching* metaphorically underscores as follows: "If you want to get rid of something, you must first allow it to flourish."

What Lao Tzu means to convey in stressing personal honesty and temporarily going to extremes with a disorder as dual means of ridding oneself of that disorder, may be epitomized in the profound truth that, as we live out our lives, we are not asked to be perfect, but rather to be what we may call "*perfectly imperfect*" as the necessary means to perfection—a point, I submit, that is the overall, albeit tacit, message of the following citations:

> True perfection seems imperfect,
> yet it is perfectly itself...
> True straightness seems crooked.
> True wisdom seems foolish.
> True art seems artless. (Poem 45)

> If you want to become whole,
> let yourself be partial.
> If you want to become straight,
> let yourself be crooked. (Poem 22)

The first passage calls us to be what I have styled "perfectly imperfect." So as to make sense of this strange-sounding "calling," let's recur to the aforementioned individual struggling with inordinate anger and impatience in consequence of her long-lasting tendency toward non-self-expression. And let's ask: What, given her *extremely* angry and impatient current condition, is this individual's most perfect course of action if she would advance beyond this condition? The perfect present course of action, the one that is perfectly appropriate for this individual at this time, is, as we've seen, to honestly own her *imperfect* psychological condition. It is, in other words, to honor herself by giving herself permission to be angry and impatient, even *extremely* angry and impatient, at this less than perfect juncture in her life. Therein lies the secret of living a "perfectly imperfect" life.

To the superficial observer, such anger and impatience will appear to be out of all due proportion, and even entirely uncalled for, as a response to a particular situation. And indeed, when compared to what we may dub "perfectly perfect" behavior, behavior that expresses the ideal response to a particular situation, such behavior plainly falls far short of the ideal mark. But this misses the central point, which is that we are not here concerned with ideal behavior per se, but with *behavior that is ideal, and therefore perfect, relative to a person's presently imperfect mental, emotional, or physical condition*. The latter, superficial assessment of this person's behavior is what Lao Tzu means to suggest, I believe, when he writes: "True straightness seems crooked. True wisdom seems foolish." However, to the more discerning observer, the "straightest" and "wisest" course of action, especially when one is in difficult straits mentally, emotionally, or physically, is almost always the seemingly "crooked" and "foolish" one of openly owning the inevitable excesses that will initially attend that course of action (about which more in Chapter 8.)

Still, when all is said and done, the 'perfectly imperfect' life is the "wisest" and "straightest" course of action because it is the shortest and most effective route to becoming physically, mentally, and emotionally whole. ("If you want to become whole, let yourself be partial [imperfect].") And the reason the 'perfectly imperfect' life is the shortest and most effective route to wholeness? Because, when all is said and done, such a life most readily and powerfully opens an individual to the Tao's healing influence, Which

> As it acts in the world...
> is like the bending of a bow.
> The top is bent downwards;
> the bottom is bent up.
> It adjusts excess and deficiency
> so that there is perfect balance. (Poem 77)

That is, the Tao, "as It acts in the world," and thus as It acts in each one of us, can't very well adjust our excesses and deficiencies, in short, our imperfections, unless we are prepared forthrightly to face up to them. And this because if, as free beings (see Poem 51), we choose not to admit our imperfections, the Tao That is Love does "not interfere" (Poem 51) with our decision, but with infinite patience and steadfastness (see above) awaits our acceptance herein, before proceeding to "adjust [our] excesses and deficiencies, so that there is perfect balance"—a "perfect balance," by the way, that signals one's realization of the Goal of goals, reunion with the Tao.

So concludes our discussion of the "way of meditation" and the "way of nature" as ways of recovering our naturally loving Tao-Nature. With respect to our review of the natural order, my contention, as indicated at the dawn of this chapter, is that, in the final rendering, nature's sundry clues to Self-recovery culminate in two essentially related, basic lessons, namely, that of letting go and that of acceptance. I shall devote Chapter 7 to the former lesson, Chapter 8 to the latter.

Notes

1. "[L]eading and not trying to control: this is the supreme virtue," states Lao Tzu (Poem 10).

2. Other Poems that cite 'non-action' as the way of the Master include Poems 2, 21, 48, and 63.

3. It should be noted that "non-action" is actually a translation of the Chinese expression usually transliterated as "*wei wu wei*." *Wei* most literally translates to "action" or "doing." *Wu* denotes a negative term, such as "not," "no," or "without." Accordingly, in its most basic sense, *wei wu wei* amounts to "action without action" or "doing without doing."

4. But why, in the final analysis, is a life beset by confusion, sorrow, and a lack of inner peace at odds with an effortless life? The answer is that as these unhappy states are effects of attachment, which is itself founded in fear, to live with confusion, sorrow, and a want of inner peace is to live one's life in the grips of fear-based distractions concerning past, present, and future occurrences, as we noticed earlier in this chapter in our discussion of meditation. In light of our present discussion, however, we may now add that to abide in a distracted state is necessarily to experience one's psychological (mental/emotional) as well physical energy as scattered, drained, and even exhausted thereby; it is to be either unable or at best less able to channel one's energy toward the realization of a specific goal, less able to exist in the meditative "Now-zone." Accordingly, a life consumed by attachment-born fear, far from being a life of effortless action, becomes instead a life fraught with stress, strain, fatigue, in a word, effort.

CHAPTER SEVEN

Nature's "Negative Lesson" for Recovering Our True Self: Letting Go

> Because he has let go,
> he can care for the people's welfare
> as a mother cares for her child.
>
> *Lao Tzu, Tao Te Ching, Poem 59*

Introduction

In Chapter 6, we surveyed various clues nature affords for recovering our true, Tao-Self. These clues included nature's call to be honest, truthful, humble, accepting, soft, yielding, flexible, and patient, both with ourselves and others, as prerequisites for recovering our True Self, along with the reminder that the signs that we have successfully recovered our True Self is a life marked by spontaneity, effortlessness, letting things take their natural course, and unflappable inner peace.

If we look closely, we cannot but notice that each of nature's "prerequisites" and "signs" herein is conditional on and presupposes a readiness to let go, and more precisely, to let go of control. For clearly, anyone who is "into" control can scarcely be expected to embrace such "prerequisites" to recovering our True Self as humility, acceptance, flexibility, and patience, much less to live a life of spontaneity, effortlessness, eagerness to let things take their natural course, and imperturbable inner peace as the unmistakable "signs" that we have in fact recovered our true, Tao-Self.

Lao Tzu's Overall Rejection of Control

But if relinquishing control is an implied condition and presupposition of the aforementioned "prerequisites" and "signs" concerning the recovery of our True Self, does Lao Tzu more expressly declare as much? He certainly does, and for starters, consider the following passages wherein Lao Tzu rejects the *overall* idea of control:

> The Master sees things as they are,
> without trying to control them.
> She lets things go their own way,
> and resides at the center of the circle. (Poem 29)
>
> The Master does his job
> and then stops.
> He understands that the universe
> is forever out of control,
> and that trying to dominate events
> goes against the current of the Tao. (Poem 30)
>
> Those who try to control,
> who use force to protect their power,
> go against the direction of the Tao. (Poem 77)
>
> The Tao nourishes by not forcing.
> By not dominating, the Master leads. (Poem 81)
>
> Because he has let go,
> he can care for the people's welfare . . . (Poem 59)

The need to control, alias to dominate, alias to force and/or, we might add, resist the issue "goes against the current of the Tao," that is, could not be more opposed to the Way of the Tao. Conversely, the Master, the one who flows with the current of the Tao, lives a life of perfect balance ("The Master does his job and then stops"), as indicated by the Master's unwillingness to control others and events. For the Master well knows that others and events have their own unique rhythms and processes (see Poem 29), and thus that, in a sense, they are "forever out of [his] control." Ultimately, by "letting things go their own way," the Master "nourishes," "leads," and "cares for the people," as he abides in a state of profound and unshakable peace ("resides at the center of the circle.")

While the latter summary of the foregoing passages clearly depicts the Master, and so the person already in possession of his or her true, Tao-Self, it no less suggests that what "goes against the current of the Tao," precisely because it goes against the current of the Tao, isn't conducive to the process of recovering our true, Tao-Self. And since trying to control others and events goes against the current of the Tao, the inescapable conclusion is that, for Lao Tzu, letting go of control is absolutely essential to the process of recovering our true, Tao-Self, as well as being supremely indicative of the Master, who has already, as it were, remade the acquaintance of her true, Tao-Self.

Still, if a disposition to control is plainly uncongenial to recovering our Tao-Self, why is it that individuals are disposed to control in the first place? What, in other words, is the underlying cause of the need to control others and events? From the perspective of the *Tao Te Ching*, the underlying cause of the urge to control, I submit, is none other than our by now old, if not good, friend, attachment, to whom we were introduced in Chapter 4.

That attachment is causally at the heart of the need to control may be inferred from the following citation:

> The Master's power is like this:
> He lets all things come and go
> effortlessly, without desire.[1]
> He never expects results;
> thus he is never disappointed. (Poem 55)

In this citation, two points are clearly connected: the Master "lets all things come and go," that is, lets go of control, because "He never expects results," that is, because he is not attached to outcomes. In other words, in this citation we learn that detachment is the causal root of a non-controlling disposition. But if so, then the implied further message is that attachment, detachment's polar opposite, is the causal root of a controlling disposition.

Granting that Lao Tzu implicitly upholds attachment as *the* causal source of controlling behavior, this gives rise to an even more pressing question: Why does Lao Tzu account attachment the causal source of controlling behavior? Truth to be told, the Sage offers no express answer to this question. Nevertheless, in light of his express causal linking of non-controlling behavior to detachment, and his implied causal linking of controlling behavior to attachment, a review of the nature, origin, and main consequence of attachment, first articulated in Chapter 4, cannot but unearth the reason Lao Tzu, however obliquely, sees fit to root controlling behavior in attached behavior.

Thus, in Chapter 4, after noting that attachment, defined as 'fear-based desire,' is itself born of the illusory belief in dualism, the belief, that is, that we exist in separation from one another, and most significantly, from the Tao, the Supreme Other, I proceeded to note that, given attachment's dualistically begotten, fear-based nature, insofar as we are beset with attachment, we will necessarily perceive others as "other," and so as "unknown," and so as "dangerous," and so as "threatening," and so, in the final analysis, as "someone or something to be feared." Or as Lao Tzu summarily puts it:

> Fear... arises from thinking of the self. (Poem 13)

Which is to say, fear arises when, and to the extent that, we regard ourselves as separate from other selves, including the Supreme Self Itself, the Tao.

In light of attachment's origin (dualism), essence (fear-based desire), and main consequence (viewing others with fear), it would seem that the need to control is a natural—if that's an appropriate term to use here—outgrowth of attachment. What we fear, be it human or otherwise, and insofar as we fear, we will seek to control either by resorting to active means or passive means. Active means of control include not only contriving to dominate others by sheer physical force; they no less, and even more insidiously, include the utilization of persuasive force, economic force, political force, and religious force. Passive means of control include passive aggressive behavior, obsessive compulsive behavior, withholding affection, ignoring, abandonment, and indifference.But whatever our controlling strategy, be it in the more active or the more passive mode, as control's invariable root is fear, the defining feature of attachment, we have a further reason, if a further reason is needed, for finding a way out of a separative-born fear-based life and into a union-born love-based life.

Lao Tzu's Rejection of Specific Modes of Control

That Lao Tzu categorically opposes control, and why he does so, is, I think we may safely say, indisputable. But he doesn't leave the matter at that; he proceeds to delineate specific modes of control that it would behoove us to let go of if we are truly intent upon recovering our true, Tao-Self. Among the modes of control that Lao Tzu urges us to relinquish, without question the first and most fundamental of them all is letting go of "self," a control-mode Lao Tzu alludes to with the question:

> When we don't see the self as self,
> what do we have to fear? (Poem 13)

As has been repeatedly maintained throughout this opus, viewed negatively, our primary spiritual task in life is to transcend the illusory belief in a separate self, to not "... see the self as self...". And why? Because to transcend belief in a separate self is to transcend attachment-spawned fear ("... what do we have to fear?"). And why is this significant? Because to transcend fear is to realize fear's contrary, unconditional love, at once the sign and experience of perfect union, communion, and accord with all that is, including, most especially, the That Which Is, "the eternal Tao."

Now, if we transcend belief in a separate self by transcending attachment-born fear, it follows that the way we overcome fear, and hence belief in a separate self, is through the practice of attachment's polar opposite, detachment. This conclusion is both logically warranted and expressly upheld by Lao Tzu when he declares:

> The Master ... is detached from all things;
> that is why she is one with them.
> Because she has let go of herself,
> she is perfectly fulfilled. (Poem 7)

The Master is one with all things—a oneness, as we've seen, whose infallible sign and experience is love—because she is detached, which is to say, because she has moved beyond fear, the unfailing sign and experience of separation. Moreover, because she is detached, and so "has let go of herself, she is perfectly fulfilled." In other words, she has achieved the pinnacle of human perfection, reunion with the Tao, and thereby, reunion with her true, loving Tao-Self.

And yet, if letting go of the illusory belief in a separate "self" is the foremost mode of letting go, there is also a secondary sense of self that it is incumbent upon us to let go of. This secondary sense of self that we need to let go of is our self-identity, our tendency to identify with, and thus to relegate ourselves to, the likes of wealth, status, physical appearance, power, intelligence, reputation, security, significant other, and so on. The main problem with any such self-identification Lao Tzu states as follows:

> He who defines himself
> can't know who he really is. (Poem 24)

That is, to identify ourselves with anything or anyone outside ourselves is, in the first place, to forget that our "True Nature" (Poem 65), our "Primal Self" (Poem 28), is divine, and, as a direct corollary of this primal act of forgetfulness, to forget as well that our value and goodness can't be found in anything or anyone outside ourselves. What is more, states Lao Tzu,

> Chase after money and security
> and your heart will never unclench.
> Care about people's approval
> and you will be their prisoner. (Poem 9)

And again,

> If you look to others for fulfillment,
> you will never truly be fulfilled.
> If your happiness depends on money,
> you will never be happy with yourself. (Poem 44)

When, and to the extent that, we forget who we truly are, and so, are moved to find our identity in things and others outside ourselves, we make ourselves things' and others' "prisoners," in that we perceive our value, goodness, and happiness to be entirely dependent upon others' "approval" and events going well in our lives. However, the sad irony in all this is that even when we receive others' approval and events are going swimmingly in our lives, we will still find ourselves incapable of loving ourselves and others (... your heart will never unclench"), with the result that "we will never be truly fulfilled" and "never be happy with ourselves."

But why is it that we will fail to love, find fulfillment in, and be happy with ourselves when, and to the extent that, we identify ourselves with anyone or anything outside ourselves? Perhaps the most obvious reason is that to so identify ourselves is a direct result of attachment to others' approval and events going well in our lives. So attached, we live with the continuously vexing fear that either others don't approve of us, or—and assuming we can allow ourselves to believe that others do approve of us—that eventually, inevitably, the other shoe will drop and we'll lose their approval.

Nor is the fear-situation any different with respect to events. Even when events do go well for us, our attachment to them going well diminishes our capacity to enjoy our success and makes us uneasily expectant that eventually, inevitably, our fortunes will change for the worse. Needless to say, to live a life fraught with the nagging fear that others don't approve of us and/or that we're destined to experience misfortune is not to live a life conducive to love of self and others, self-fulfillment, and self-happiness.

The less obvious, more radical reason why such self-identification doesn't contribute to happiness is that it amounts to an act of profound self-rejection. To so identify ourselves is to send ourselves, whether consciously or unconsciously, the self-negating message that we're not good and valuable, or at least, not *that* good and valuable, in ourselves, and hence, that we need to find our value and goodness in and through something or someone other than ourselves. Eventually, especially if this message is of sufficient duration and intensity, we will come to believe it. Which belief is but a short step away from an even more pernicious belief that we come to accept about ourselves, namely, that, given our inherent non-value and non-goodness, we're unworthy of physical, psychological, and relational happiness. And, when, and to the extent that, we come to accept this latter belief about ourselves, we will begin to manifest our "unworthiness of happiness" in the way of varying kinds and degrees of physical, psychological, and relational disorders. Whence, the more radical reason why seeking our identity in and through anyone or anything outside ourselves is a quest that cannot but lead to greatly diminished self-love, desperate unfulfillment, and, as a result, unhappiness with ourselves.

Another mode of control Lao Tzu bids us let go of is the need to interfere. For,

> True mastery can be gained
> by letting things go their own way.
> It can't be gained by interfering. (Poem 48)

This passage reiterates Lao Tzu's view that the true Master lets go of control, save that it intimates that the heart of letting go is the art of non-interference. I say the "art of non-interference" because, in fact, being a practitioner of non-interference isn't so much a science as it is a skill arising from the exercise of the Master's intuitive faculty.

In Chapter 5, we determined that intuitive knowing, a function of our connection to the Tao, is a direct and immediate insight into a person or event that enables us to make the appropriate decision in a given situation. Moreover, we specifically labeled this ability to make appropriate decisions in a given situation via the exercise of our intuitive faculty "wisdom," since wisdom *is* the appropriate application of knowledge in a given situation. Accordingly, anyone skilled in the art of non-interference is necessarily a highly intuitive, and hence, extraordinarily wise, individual.

But why is the practice of non-interference conditional on wisdom, the appropriate application of knowledge in a given situation? Lao Tzu intimates an answer when he writes that the Tao, and by implication, the Master, "guides without interfering" (Poem 51), that is, strikes the delicate balance between guidance and interference. We strike this ever-so delicate balance when, instead of contriving to force our beliefs, opinions, lifestyle, profession, etc., upon others, we take individuals where they are physically, mentally, emotionally, and spiritually *at the time* and offer advice based on their present stage of development. A prime indicator that such advice is truly wise advice is a readiness to let individuals learn their own lessons at their own pace, while at the same time discerning when they may require more or less supportive, not intrusive, intervention as they proceed at their own learning pace. For the truly wise Master is profoundly aware that,

> There is a time for being ahead,
> a time for being behind;
> a time for being in motion,
> a time for being at rest . . . (Poem 29)

As I have said, guidance in this sense can't be an exact science, can't simply be a matter of applying a general rule to a particular case (see Chapter 5), but presupposes individuals possessed of great intuitive sensitivity, and hence, wisdom, the fitting application of knowledge in a given, here and now situation. Such guidance, it goes without saying, is, and can only be, the province of the Master, the true practitioner of the art of non-interference, of letting things and people go their own way.

In another passage, Lao Tzu exhorts us to "Stop trying to control" in two further ways, when he writes:

> Let go of fixed plans and concepts,
> and the world will govern itself. (Poem 57)

First, let's consider the problematic status of cleaving to "*fixed* plans." I highlight the modifier "fixed" herein so as to call attention to what Lao Tzu is not suggesting we let go of. He is not suggesting that we let go of making plans per se, only that we let go of immutable, dogmatically held plans. In fact, and as we noticed in Chapter 3, even "the eternal Tao" from the beginning works from a "plan," namely, Its Conceptual Yin/Yang Design for creation. And in Chapter 6 we learned that the natural order is governed by certain preordained natural laws, which is to say, by a comprehensive plan of operation that is itself derived from and a reflection of the Tao's eternal Nature.

Still, if it seems apparent that even the Great Tao works from a plan, what are we to make of Lao Tzu's assertion in Poem 73 that "The Tao . . . accomplishes without a plan"? Doesn't this assertion flatly contradict my contention that the Tao works from a plan? My answer is that in fact said assertion *cannot* deny what I have contended herein, for the very compelling reason that to so deny would place Lao Tzu in contradiction with himself! As was just noted, both Chapters 3 and 6 reveal that the Tao works from a Self-conceived plan that mirrors the Tao's eternal Nature. Therefore, when Lao Tzu asserts that "The Tao . . . accomplishes without a plan," he must intend thereby something other than the proposition that the Tao is absolutely plan*less*.

I submit that Poem 51 holds the key to unraveling Lao Tzu's true intent when he declares that "The Tao . . . accomplishes without a plan." Recall that this Poem compactly profiles the Tao's creative activity. Among other things, it notes that the Tao's created Self-expressions are created "free," and that the Tao

creates without possessing,
acts without expecting,
guides without interfering.[2]

As is all-too evident from these citations, the Creator Tao gives almost unlimited self-expressive leeway to Its free Self-expressions. In so doing, the Tao can't possibly have a "fixed plan," a fixed agenda and timetable, for each of Its free created forms. In the vernacular of the day, we might say that, in light of the freedom the Tao accords certain of Its Self-expressions and Its resultant policy of non-interference, the Tao has no choice but to "hang loose" with respect to Its freedom-endowed creations, and, as we learned in Chapter 6, to wait in patience and steadfastness until such time as they willingly allow the Tao to "... adjust [their] excesses and deficiencies." For the Tao well knows that, in the fullness of time,

The hard and the stiff will be broken.
The soft and supple will prevail. (Poem 76)

The Tao, in other words, is well aware that, eventually, ineluctably, all of Its created forms will remember who they truly are, divine Self-expressions of the Tao Itself, at which fully recollective point the prophetic words of the *Tao Te Ching* will be fulfilled:

All things end in the Tao
as rivers flow into the sea. (Poem 32)

My contention, then, is that when Lao Tzu says that "The Tao ... accomplishes without a plan," he means without a "*fixed* plan." The Tao's ultimate plan or goal is reunion with Itself, the specific processes Its free created forms go through and the time it takes to realize this goal, is, given their inherent freedom, a matter of personal choice. Not that the Tao entirely abandons Its created forms to their own processes and timetables. Let's not forget that,

> The Tao's net covers the whole universe.
> And though its meshes are wide,
> it doesn't let a thing slip through. (Poem 73)

In that Its created forms are immanent manifestations of the Tao, the transcendent Tao could not abandon them even if it wanted to, since to do so would be to abandon Itself! No, *qua* immanent, the Tao is intimately involved in Its forms' lives and times, not in the manner of a controlling overlord, but rather in the manner of an unconditionally loving "Mother" Who ceaselessly "nourishes," "maintains," "cares for," "comforts," "protects," and "guides" Her children "without interfering" in their lives and times (see Poem 51).

Therefore, we might, in the interest of precision and clarity, if not of poetic brevity and elegance, amend Lao Tzu's statement that "The Tao ... accomplishes without a plan" to read: "The Tao [inevitably] accomplishes [Its ultimate purpose for Its created Self-expressions] without a [fixed] plan."

If the foregoing accurately portrays the Tao's 'planned activity,' then, as the Tao is our Supreme Model, the natural, and so, the most expedient, course of action for us is, like the Tao, to eschew "fixed plans." But to maintain that having fixed plans is not in keeping with the Tao, and therefore not in keeping with the natural order and expediency, leaves unanswered exactly why this is so. And the answer, not surprisingly, is that the impulse to cleave to fixed plans bespeaks a form of control, to wit, the attempt to control the future, the problematic status of which Lao Tzu puts metaphorically as follows:

> Trying to control the future
> is like trying to take the master carpenter's place.
> When you handle the master carpenter's tools,
> chances are that you'll cut yourself. (Poem 74)

In this citation, the "master carpenter" represents the Tao, the "master carpenter's tools," the Tao's overall plan of reunion with Itself, "handling the master carpenter's tools," the attempt to replace the

Tao's overall plan with our own "fixed plans," and "cutting ourselves," the sorrow, confusion, and lack of inner peace that are the unhappy issue of stubborn adherence to our fixed plans.

More to the point, we will suffer as a result of our clinging to fixed plans precisely because such clinging, as a mode of control, stems from fear-based attachment. As such, to have fixed plans is to live in constant fear either that we won't attain our goal, or if we do happen to attain our goal, that we won't be able to retain it. To hold fast to fixed plans, in other words, all but guarantees a life plagued by attachment-spawned sorrow and confusion, which is only to say, a life of suffering.

To avoid such attachment-derived suffering, we need, like the Tao, to "hang loose" with our plans, a point Lao Tzu alludes to in the following passages:

> A good traveler has no fixed plans,
> and is not intent upon arriving. (Poem 27)
>
> The Master allows things to happen.
> She shapes events as they come.
> She steps out of the way
> and lets the Tao speak for itself. (Poem 45)
>
> The Master ... lets himself be shaped by the
> Tao ... (Poem 39)

The fact of the matter is that, due to the "Fall," we're largely, though certainly not entirely, bound by the laws of time and space. We don't see the whole space-time picture, no matter how gifted we are clairvoyantly, precognitively, and retrocognitively! Not so, as we've seen, "the eternal Tao," for Whom past, present, and future give way to the space and time-transcending "Now."[3] For this reason, to clutch doggedly to our "fixed plan" is to fail to enjoy and appreciate our unique life-journey ("A good traveler has no fixed plans, and is not intent upon arriving"), as well as to risk missing the Tao's, to say the least, higher-perspective-born inner guidance ("The Master ... lets himself be shaped by the Tao"), which just may be calling us to "step out of [our own] way," and embrace a new life-plan and -goal.

But if our challenge is to tread lightly with our plans and to be open to the Tao's wise inner promptings, is there any discernible way of knowing that we are truly hearing the Tao's voice, or, as Western religion is wont to put it, that we are truly doing God's will? As a matter of fact, the infallible sign that we are verily in tune with the Tao has already been indirectly indicated in this and the preceding chapter, which sign may be expressed in either negative or positive terms. The negative sign is that,

> In the practice of the Tao …
> Less and less do you need to force things,
> until finally you arrive at non-action. (Poem 48)

As to the positive indicator of attunement to the Tao, Lao Tzu writes:

> The Master's power is like this.
> He lets all things come and go
> effortlessly, without desire.
> He never expects results;
> thus he is never disappointed. (Poem 55)[4]

The negative sign that our plans and the Tao's plans are in accord is an unwillingness "to force things," an unwillingness culminating in "non-action" (see Chapter 6). The positive sign herein is a life lived with effortlessness, culminating in perfect detachment. Were we to combine both signs into a single sign, we might say that collectively they signify a life wherein struggle is virtually a forgotten word, never to be heard from again. In other words, we should ever bear in mind that

> The great Way is easy,
> yet people prefer the side paths.
> Be aware when things are out of balance.
> Stay centered within the Tao. (Poem 53)5

To recur to yet another notion discussed in Chapter 6, we know "when things are out of balance," and so, not "centered within the Tao," when our "way" isn't easy. On the other hand, we know when things are in balance, and so, centered in the Tao, when our "way," like "The great Way, is easy." Then and only then will the truth of Lao Tzu's words,

> Be content with what you have;
> rejoice in the way things are.
> When you realize there is nothing lacking,
> the whole world belongs to you. (Poem 44),

be fully realized in our lives.

A related "fixation" Lao Tzu would have us let go of is that of "*fixed* concepts." Again, note that, as with "fixed plans," Lao Tzu is not, nor can he be, suggesting that we abandon concepts per se, only that we let go of the penchant for "fixed concepts." That the Sage can't be suggesting an out-and-out relinquishing of conceptualization is perhaps most apparent from the fact that conceptualization, as was shown in Chapter 1, is at the heart of human categorical knowing, propositional language, and reasoning—in other words, at the heart of normal* human understanding and communication as such. Accordingly, as letting go of concepts altogether would require nothing less than the letting go of human nature itself, it seems highly unlikely that Lao Tzu has this sort of letting go in mind when he bids us let go of "fixed concepts." Nevertheless, if concepts are indispensable to human knowing, this isn't to say that they don't have their cognitive drawbacks. In Chapter 1, we also discussed concepts' inadequacy as cognitive links to and representations of the Tao. Indeed, we observed that it is concepts' very strength, their classifying and distinguishing function,

---

*I say "normal human knowing and communication." Perhaps a more apt expression would be "*more overt* human knowing and communication," since, as we gathered from Chapter 5, intuitive knowing, while no less a part of human knowing and communication, is far less recognizably so.

that ultimately renders them inadequate as cognitive signifiers of the Tao that, *qua* formless, transcends all delimiting classifications and distinctions. It is primarily for this reason, I submit, that Lao Tzu asks us to let go of "fixed concepts." For, to hold fast to fixed concepts about the Tao, is to fail to appreciate that,

> The Tao is ungraspable.
> How can her mind be at one with it?
> Because she doesn't cling to ideas. (Poem 21)

But to assert that "The Tao is ungraspable" is not to assert that the Tao entirely exceeds our conceptual ken. In Chapter 1, I no less stressed the point that, among the Tao's attributes, "formlessness" ranks first in importance. First in importance because only a formless Reality, only a Reality beyond all classification, distinction, and composition, can be termed perfect, infinite, unchanging, eternal, and absolutely unique. For this reason, I went on to show—and here I will but state the conclusion of a rather lengthy analysis—that we can make true, meaningful, and absolutely unique affirmations about the Tao, such as "The Tao, and the Tao alone, is formless," "The Tao, and the Tao alone, is infinite," while at the same time maintaining that the Tao is beyond our classifying and distinguishing conceptual grasp.

Next, in Chapter 1, but especially in Chapter 5, I pointed out that, if in fact "The Tao is [conceptually] ungraspable," the only way "our minds [can] be at one with it" is by not "clinging to ideas," and establishing a direct and immediate, in a word, intuitive, connection with the Tao. When we can "step back from our own mind" and thereby realize an intuitive connection with the Tao, writes Lao Tzu, we will acquire an "understanding of all things." (Poem 10) An "understanding of all things," not in the sense that we become omniscient beings, since only the transcendent, eternal Tao is truly omniscient. Rather, we acquire an "understanding of all things" in the sense that, to so connect with the Tao, is to realize a deeper, richer love-knowledge of the Tao (see Chapter 5), and insofar, both to know what is, and to be able to perform, the appropriately loving action in a given, here and now situation. In brief, to so connect with the Tao makes of us not just loving individuals, but even more profoundly, *wisely loving individuals*.

In a similar, albeit less epistemological and metaphysical, vein, to forget that "The Tao is ungraspable" by dint of cleaving to "fixed concepts" is effectively to reduce the Tao to our own personal concepts, beliefs, and experiences, and even to our own purportedly "revealed" concepts, beliefs, and experiences, which is to say, to the tenets of a particular religious persuasion. Actually, some such reduction of the Tao is inevitable, given our human reliance on conceptual knowing, as we've oft noticed. The danger lies in regarding our reduction not as what it is, only *our* reduction, but as verily *the* reduction. Aside from aiding and abetting a dualistically driven "I-other" mentality, with all that that abusively entails (see Chapter 6), to regard our reduction as *the* reduction fails to take into account that "The Tao follows only itself" (Poem 25), that the formless, eternal, and infinite Tao can't be confined to and defined by our concepts, beliefs, and experiences. It is, once again, to fail to allow the Tao to be the Tao, to presume to be privy to both the Tao's Own mind and plan of operation in our and all others' lives. It is, in the final analysis, to acquit ourselves in the very unTao-like manner of trying, whether wittingly or no, to control the ways and means of "The Tao [that] follows only itself."

Then again, when Lao Tzu asks,

> Can you coax your mind from its wandering
> and keep to the original oneness? (Poem 10),

he would have us "let go of fixed ... concepts" for an even more profound reason: a mind fixated on concepts, whether in the guise of reasoning, remembering, imagining, daydreaming, or whatever, is a "wandering," and therefore non-meditative mind. The Reader will recall our discussion of meditation in Chapter 6. There, we saw that meditation essentially consists of a state of undistracted focus for a positive purpose. Such positive focusing places the meditator, even if temporarily, beyond the clutches of fear-based distractions concerning the past, present, and future, and in the Now or the Moment, thereby establishing the meditator in experiential communion with the eternal Tao Itself. Lao Tzu's point in the foregoing passage, then, is to remind us that a "wandering," concept-laden mind is a mind that will fail of communion with the eternal Tao, or, as he puts it, fail to "keep to the original oneness," and, insofar, fail to reap the inestimable physical, psychological, and spiritual harvest that are the fruits of that communion, that "oneness."

Yet another good reason to let go of fixed concepts follows from the existential fact that,

> Trying to grasp things, you lose them. (Poem 64)

To reduce things to our conceptual "grasp" is to "lose them." It is to "lose them" in the sense that to so reduce things is to lose sight of the truth that each and every thing is a *unique* Self-manifestation of the Tao, and hence beyond conceptual categorization and distinction. Which is not to say, be it noted, that individuals are *entirely* beyond conceptual categorization. As we learned in Chapter 1, when, say, we know that someone's name is "Susie," we no less know that this individual is a *female human being*. Knowing this about Susie means that we know that she is a member of the class, "female human being," as well as that her class is distinct from other classes of individuals, human or otherwise. But to know that Susie belongs to this class of individuals that is distinct from other classes of individuals is not to know Susie *qua* individual. *Qua* individual, Susie is and will e'er remain opaque to conceptual knowing, and for that reason a singularly mysterious Self-manifestation of the *Mysterium Mysteriorum*, the eternal Tao.

As a final, more practical inducement to let go of fixed concepts, Lao Tzu points out that,

> The mark of a moderate man
> is freedom from his own ideas.

> Tolerant like the sky...
> supple like a tree in the wind,
> he has no destination in view
> and makes use of anything
> life happens to bring his way. (Poem 59)

Earlier in this chapter, I had occasion to note that a prime mark of the Master is a balanced life, and why. Now, Lao Tzu continues this theme of balance by observing that "The mark of the moderate [balanced] man is freedom from his own ideas." The moderate/balanced man is free from his own ideas because he is detached ("he has no destination in view") from his ideas, beliefs, point of view, opinions, and so on. So detached, the moderate/balanced man has no need to control his and others' ideas, beliefs, etc., much less to control his and others' lives. Otherwise put, the moderate/balanced man's keynotes are "tolerance" toward others' views and flexibility ("suppleness") with respect to his own views. For the moderate/balanced man, attuned to the Way of the Tao, knows full well that the Tao's Way isn't necessarily his way ("The Tao follows only itself." [Poem 25]), so that when change and its mercurial children, novelty, spontaneity, and unpredictability, occur in his life, he is never dismayed. He is sustained by the unshakeable conviction that "The great Way is easy..." (Poem 53), and that change-wrought discomfort due to his own ideas, beliefs, etc., means that he is out of attunement, out of balance with the Tao, and thus that his old ideas, beliefs, etc., are no longer in keeping with his highest good.

On a more positive note, the moderate/balanced man is profoundly aware that change-wrought discomfort due to his own ideas, beliefs, etc., is the Tao's clarion call to new life, to higher levels of psychological and spiritual growth. For this reason, the moderate/balanced man doesn't resist change by clinging tenaciously to his outmoded ideas, beliefs, etc., but rather "makes use of anything life happens to bring his way," by willingly, even gratefully, adapting his ideas, beliefs, etc., to his new, more life-giving, *Tao-given*, circumstances. So does the moderate/balanced man pave the way for the attainment of the ultimate spiritual prize: the recovery of his true, loving, Tao-Nature.

And so too does this conclude our discussion of nature's negative lesson for recovering our true, Tao-Nature: letting go of control. Now, I have chosen to label letting go of control nature's "negative lesson" for recovering our True Nature, because, while this lesson is certainly instructive, insightful, and in many ways helpful toward achieving our Self-recovering goal, it tells us only that the way we let go of the urge to control ourselves, others, and events is through the conquering of attachment, the source of this urge. Left unstated are the particulars of how we go about conquering attachment, overcoming the need to control, and, for our efforts, gaining the prize of prizes, the recovery of our True Nature. For the particulars of Lao Tzu's more positive, nature-inspired answer to the all-important question of how we may recover our True Nature, I offer for your discerning consideration this book's penultimate chapter 8.

Notes

1. As noted in Chapter 4, footnote 1, the expression "without desire," or the equivalent thereof, e.g., "desirelessness," is frequently, and in my opinion, wrongly used in spiritual literature as a synonym for detachment, just as the expression "desire," or the equivalent thereof, is frequently, and in my opinion, wrongly used in spiritual literature as a synonym for attachment. In Chapter 8, I shall show why these expressions fail to convey the true meaning of detachment and attachment, respectively.

2. As to our freedom to express ourselves, Lao Tzu also writes: "The Tao is always present within you. You can use it any way you want." (Poem 6)

3. As the Tao lives in the "Now" and is cognizant of the whole picture, so the Master, as the embodiment of the Tao, "... gives himself up to whatever the moment brings" (Poem 50), and "... views the parts with compassion, because he understands the whole." (Poem 39)

4. This same theme of effortlessness and non-attachment Lao Tzu also states, albeit not as explicitly as in Poem 55, in these concise terms: "If you want to accord with the Tao, just do your job, then let go." (Poem 24)

5. Much in this same non-struggling spirit, Lao Tzu writes: "If you let yourself be blown to and fro, you lose touch with your root. If you let restlessness move you, you lose touch with who you are." (Poem 26)

CHAPTER EIGHT

Nature's "Positive Lesson" for Recovering Our True Self: Acceptance

If you accept the world...
you will return to your primal self.
Lao Tzu, Tao Te Ching, Poem 28

Introduction

I concluded Chapter 7 by noting that it remains to be shown how Lao Tzu suggests we go about overcoming *the* impediment to recovering our True Nature, attachment. I also said that the answer to this crucial question is nature's "positive lesson" for recovering our True Nature. That answer, as the title of this chapter reveals, is acceptance.

However, before attempting to justify this answer, it will be necessary to clear up a problem that I referred to in footnote 1 of Chapter 4. The problem in question is "an age-old misconception [that] continues to haunt the notions of attachment and detachment," namely, "the tendency among both Eastern and Western spiritual thinkers... to equate attachment with desire and detachment with sheer desirelessness." In that same note I went on to say that I would reserve critical comment on this misreading of attachment and detachment for Chapter 8, but that, until that fateful chapter, I would leave the matter of the meaning of detachment in abeyance and accept, without attempting to justify, Prabhavananda and Isherwood's definition of attachment as 'fear-based desire.'

Accordingly, before proceeding to argue that nature's positive lesson of acceptance is the antidote to attachment, it will be necessary to (1) show why the all-but universal habit of identifying attachment with desire and detachment with desirelessness is an erroneous identification, and (2) indicate the true meaning of attachment and detachment.

Against the Attachment as Desire, Detachment as Desirelessness, Equations

Unfortunately, virtually all translators of the *Tao Te Ching*, as well as translators of other past and present spiritual classics, have tended to identify attachment with desire and detachment with desirelessness. And no exception to this tendency is Dr. Stephen Mitchell, whose otherwise superb translation of the *Tao Te Ching* yours truly has utilized in this book. I have seen fit to work from Dr. Mitchell's translation because, as I noted in the Introduction, I am convinced that he, perhaps more than anyone else, manages both "to strike the delicate interpretive balance between modernity and antiquity..." and to "capture *the* message of the *Tao Te Ching*, namely, that acceptance, and in particular, self-acceptance," is the spiritual "key to recovering our True, Tao-Nature." Still, if we can find some niggling fault with even the great works of art, then perhaps Dr. Mitchell will forgive me when I cite such passages as,

> Free from desire, you realize the mystery.
> Caught in desire, you see only the manifestations.
> (Poem 1)
>
> When there is no desire,
> all things are at peace. (Poem 37)
>
> The Master... lets all things come and go...
> without desire. (Poem 55),

and propose that desire and desirelessness as time-honored synonyms for attachment and detachment, respectively, are inadequate, and for two principal reasons, one logical, the other commonsensical.

By logically inadequate herein I allude to the fact that though spiritual writers are generally of like mind in equating desire with attachment and desirelessness with detachment, occasionally we find them in contradiction among, and even with, themselves on this equational score. To see what I mean, first consider the following sample statements fully in support of said equations.

Thus, in the *The Upanishads* (ca. 800 BCE), the culminating Vedic scriptures of Hinduism, we find this verse: "When are liberated all the desires that lodge in one's heart, then a mortal becomes an immortal! Therein he reaches *Brahman* [the Godhead]!"[1] In this same vein, Christian mystic, Meister Eckhart (1260–1327), puts the case against desire and for desirelessness in these emphatic terms: "[A]s long as you have the will, even the will to fulfill God's will, and as long as you have the desire for eternity and for God, to this very extent you are not properly poor, for the only one who is a poor person is one who wills nothing and desires nothing."[2] Another Christian mystic, Saint John of the Cross (1542–1592), for his part, makes explicit the tendency to equate detachment with desirelessness, and by implication attachment with desire, when he writes: "It is impossible for the will to attain to the sweetness and bliss of the divine union otherwise than in detachment, in refusing to the desire every pleasure in the things of heaven and earth."[3] And as a final example, Aldous Huxley epitomizes the common Eastern and Western view that attachment is all one with desire, detachment with desirelessness, succinctly as follows: "Desirelessness is the condition of deliverance and illumination."[4]

So far, so good. But now ponder, if you will, four further sample citations, the first two of which, interestingly enough, are also from the erst-mentioned *Upanishads*: "The Self [*Brahman* immanent, namely, *Atman*], which is free from evil, ageless, deathless, sorrowless, hungerless, thirstless ... He should be searched out, Him one should desire to understand. He obtains all worlds and all desires who has found out and who understands that Self."[5] And: "He who is without desire, who is freed from desire ... whose desire is the Self ... Being very Brahman, he goes to Brahman."[6] The third example is found in our very own *Tao*

Te Ching, wherein we read, for example, "Free from desire, you realize the mystery" (Poem 1), only to be advised thereafter that, "What the Master desires is non-desire." (Poem 64) The fourth and final example is excerpted from Sri Swami Satchidananda's commentary on yet another Hindu spiritual classic, *The Yoga Sutras of Patanjali*. After noting that, "The *Vedantic* scriptures say: 'Even the desire for liberation is a bondage.' *Mokshabheksho bandhaha*: 'Even if you desire liberation, you are binding yourself. Every desire binds you and brings restlessness. To get the liberation you have to be completely desireless'", in the very next paragraph Swami Satchidananda goes on to remark: "Is it possible to be desireless? No. Actually, it is not possible. As long as the mind is there, its duty is to desire. It seems to be contradictory. But the secret is that any desire without any personal or selfish motive will never bind you. Why? Because the pure, selfless desire has no expectations whatsoever, so it knows no disappointment."[7]

What are we to make of the preceding citations, the first of which evidently contradicts those earlier citations that expressly frown on desire and promote desirelessness as the royal road back to the divine, while the second, third and fourth of which unequivocally contradict themselves in that they first plainly reject desire in favor of desirelessness, after which they just as plainly reinstate desire as the desirable vehicle for reunion with the Source! Is there any way to reconcile such seemingly irreconcilable views on the appropriateness of desire in our quest for reunion with the Source?

I believe there is such a way, and to this conciliatory end, let me begin by flatly asserting that those authors who equate desire with attachment, desirelessness with detachment, are either simply wrong, or else intend by desire and desirelessness something other than what these terms *literally* denote. Which brings me to my commensensical objection to these would-be equations, namely, were we devoid of all desire, of all wanting, we would lack any and all motivation to quest after the Godhead Itself! Indeed, the last cited passages from the *Upanishads* implicitly assert this very thing when they declare: "The Self... should be searched out, Him one should desire to understand," and "He... whose desire is the Self... Being very Brahman, he goes to Brahman."

What is more, as such a quest evidently demands that we be somewhat sound physically and psychologically, lest our energies be dissipated in dealing with our mental, emotional, and physical afflictions, it would seem that, preliminary to, and as a prime condition of, desiring the Godhead Itself, we should be no less desirous of our own physical and psychological health and well-being. In which case, it becomes equally apparent that we should desire for ourselves such things as good, wholesome food, proper exercise, sufficient rest and relaxation, adequate mental and emotional stimulation, and, in general, a balanced life physically, mentally, and emotionally.

In short, that the historic attachment as desire, detachment as desirelessness equations should give us pause is clear both from the fact that contradictory claims have and continue to be made as to the desirability of desire in pursuit of the Source (the logical objection), and, even more compellingly, I believe, from the self-evident observation that, devoid of desire, we would lack the will, the motivation, to pursue the very Godhead that these same spiritual texts exhort us to pursue (the commonsense objection!)

Attachment as "Fear-Based Desire" Revisited

Largely for these reasons, then, I favor Swami Prabhavananda and Christopher Isherwood's characterization of attachment as desire qualified by fear, or fear-based desire. The issue isn't desire as such, but, as I have repeatedly stated, fear. It is fear that we need to overcome if we are to rid ourselves of attachment. It is fear that signals our illusory separation from the Tao and the Tao's Self-manifestations, and gives rise to the three primal afflictions, sorrow, confusion, and a want of inner peace. It is fear that is the source of our need to control ourselves, others, and events. It is fear that causes us to doubt and fret over the realization of a much-desired outcome, and even, should we realize this outcome, unremittingly haunts us with the bleak conviction that, sooner or later, we are bound, and even deserve!, to lose it. In short, it is primarily, if not exclusively, due to fear-based desire, not desire per se, that our lives are rent with suffering, physically, psychologically, and spiritually (see especially Chapters 4 and 7).

But let's not be too hasty here. Is it necessarily fear that fundamentally qualifies desire as attachment? Granting that desire isn't itself identifiable with attachment, might there not be another, even more fundamentally qualifying attribute than fear at the heart of attachment? Could it not be, as some spiritual writers hold, that attachment is better defined, not as fear-based desire, but rather as "*selfish* desire?" A case in point, the aforementioned Swami Satchidananda, according to whom (what we may style) 'good desire' is the selfsame as "*selfless* desire." Such desire, he effectively argues, is good (notwithstanding his firm asseveration in the previous paragraph that the goal is to become "completely desireless.") This evident discrepancy notwithstanding, for Swami Satchidananda, it is selfishness, not fear, that is the specifically qualifying attribute of desire that generates attachment, since it is due to selfish desire that we have expectations, obsess over and doubt the realization of a desired outcome, and experience disappointment when we fail to attain a desired outcome.

In opposition to the view that selfishness is the true cause of attachment, I would contend that selfishness is rather a prime symptom, an effect of the true cause. And the true cause of selfish inclinations and behavior? It is, I submit, and as Prabhavananda and Isherwood indicate, precisely fear. For doesn't it stand well to reason that the more internally racked we are with fear, the more self-absorbed we will be, and so, the less aware of and sensitive to other persons, things, and situations, and the more apt to use and abuse other persons, things, and situations?

Fear-beset individuals exist, so to speak, with their eyes turned ceaselessly back upon themselves, a reflective gaze that renders them self-conscious in the extreme. Self-consciously fixated upon their own fear-driven cares and preoccupations, they find themselves far less capable of looking out *to* and *for* others, of opening freely, spontaneously, and lovingly to others, and of appreciating life's myriad wonders, riches, and possibilities.

Furthermore, self-conscious extremists discover that fear not only renders them self-absorbed and desensitizes them to other persons, things, and life in general; it no less constricts their ability to express their own true feelings, thoughts, and desires. And this because insofar as they are burdened with fear, they cannot but doubt themselves, doubt their potential, their ability, their choices, their instincts, their feelings and desires. Again, insofar as they fear, and so doubt themselves, they become ever more susceptible to and reliant upon the approval of others in order to approve of themselves. Ultimately, insofar as they fear, and so doubt themselves, "they begin to depend upon authority" (see Poem 72) for approbation and their sense of self-worth, and especially upon that authoritative triumvirate of morality, religion, and law (see Chapter 5).

In sum, because fear spawns "self-absorption," "self-conscious extremism," and "insensitivity to other persons, things, and situations," fear is the primal cause of selfishness. And because fear inhibits our freedom, spontaneity, and capacity to enjoy life, as well as fosters self-doubt and the resultant slavish dependence upon others, especially authoritative others, for approbation and our sense of self-worth, fear is also the prime causal source of our predisposition to agonize over and doubt the realization of a desired outcome, of our disappointment when we fail to attain a desired outcome, and, even when we do attain it, of our inability to enjoy it, so vexed are we by the prospect of losing it.

Whence, my contention that fear, not selfishness, is the prime distinguishing component of attachment, and that, as such, 'fear-based desire', as Prabhavananda and Isherwood suggest, more accurately, clearly, and fundamentally captures the unwholesome essence of attachment than does "selfish desire."

"Fearless Desire" as "Ideal Attachment"

So much for attachment, which, I have argued, is best defined as 'fear-based desire.' If this stands as a good definition of attachment, what would be a correspondingly good definition of attachment's polar opposite, detachment, the practice of which, spiritual writers all but universally proclaim, is the supreme condition of reunion with the Source?

Perhaps the strongest definitional temptation here is to draw the eminently logical conclusion that, if attachment amounts to 'fear-based desire', detachment, by contrast, must boil down to 'fearless desire'. The advantage in so defining detachment is that it escapes the historically sanctioned penchant of regarding detachment as unqualified desirelessness, the difficulties with which I have above remarked on. But on analysis, this would-be advantage soon shows itself to be unworkable in the extreme. To equate detachment with 'fearless desire' would mean that our desires, being devoid of fear, the antithesis of love, are perfectly loving desires, and, because perfect love is at once the sign and experience of perfect union, that we have realized perfect union with the Source that is Love Itself (see Chapter 4). The reason the detachment-as-fearless-desire-equation is unworkable, then, is that it entails the (drolly) contradictory claim that we would already have to be in union with the Source before we could strive to be in union with the Source! Plainly, detachment, so regarded, can in no way serve as the claimed means to union with the Source, since it *presupposes* a state of realized union with Source.

Which is not to say that we must reject altogether the detachment-as-fearless-desire-equation. Actually, this equation has its place just so long as we understand it to express, however obliquely, the *ideal* state of detachment, or if you will, 'ideal detachment', and for the following reason: If 'fearless desire' is synonymous with 'perfectly loving desire,' and 'perfectly loving desire' bespeaks a state of perfect union with the Source, then 'fearless desire' may be said to articulate, however circuitously, the ideal state and ultimate goal of detachment.

Still, even granting the ideal status of the detachment-as-fearless-desire-equation, the ironic fact is that this equation is even less helpful than the previously rejected detachment-as-desirelessness-equation as a procedural indicator of how we are to overcome attachment and thereby, realize union with the Source! Time now to reintroduce Lao Tzu into the discussion, and in particular, his positive lesson of nature, acceptance, for therein, I shall argue, lies the answer to the riddle of what detachment *practically* is and how its practice effects reunion with the Source That is Love, and, for good measure, the recovery of our True Nature.

But any such argument presupposes the legitimacy of my claim that Lao Tzu regards acceptance as nature's positive lesson for recovering our True Nature. That acceptance verily is Lao Tzu's candidate for nature's positive lesson is verifiable, I believe, both on logical and textual grounds.

Acceptance as Nature's Positive Lesson for Recovering Our True Nature: The Evidence

In Chapter 7, I argued in sundry ways that letting go of control is, for Lao Tzu, nature's negative lesson for recovering our True Nature. Assuming the rightfulness of these arguments, it becomes evident, even logically evident, that the positive flip side of letting go of control (as a negative indicator of how we go about recovering our True Nature) is acceptance. Indeed, it goes without saying that to be able let go of the need to control ourselves, others, and events entails acceptance of ourselves, others, and events. Thus, the need to control others' lives underscores our unwillingness to accept them as they are; the need to control ourselves, say, by reining in our spontaneity, denotes our unwillingness to accept ourselves as we truly are; and the need to control events, say, by fudging on our finances, signals our unwillingness to accept our present financial reality. Suffice it to say for now, then, that, logically speaking, acceptance is the positive counterpart to the negative injunction to relinquish control

But beyond logicality, does Lao Tzu give us any specific textual reason to conclude that he accounts acceptance nature's positive lesson for recovering our True Nature? In fact, he provides unequivocal evidence when he writes:

> [A]ccept the world as it is.
> If you accept the world,
> the Tao will be luminous inside you
> and you will return to your primal self. (Poem 28)

The point could not be clearer: acceptance of the way things are begets reunion with the Tao ("the Tao will be luminous inside you") and the recovery of our True Nature ("primal self"). But since reuniting with the Tao and recovering our True Nature presuppose the conquering of attachment, and conquering attachment hinges on detachment, this passage further implies that acceptance is Lao Tzu's answer to what I have labeled 'practical (as opposed to ideal) detachment', that is, detachment whose practice serves as a viable means of overcoming attachment and realizing in the bargain reunion with the Tao and the recovery of our True Nature. But the view that practical detachment is the selfsame as acceptance is much too important to rest on an implied justification thereto. Accordingly, let's see if there might not be more explicit, and thus compelling, reasons in support of my contention that Lao Tzu upholds the acceptance/practical detachment equation.

Acceptance: The Way Back to Our True Nature

Above, we saw that if detachment is to serve as a practicable means of recovering our True Nature it must take into account one painfully apparent fact about human beings, which is that the vast majority of them are attached, and thus find themselves more or less in the grip of assorted fears. Given this fear-burdened human condition, the question, as far as detachment is concerned, comes down to this: *How do we practice detachment despite and in the face of our attached, fear-ridden condition?* And my answer, as I have indicated, is by practicing "practical detachment," by which I understand the practice of acceptance. But permit me to explain.

To begin with, I would remind the Reader of several of the main points made in Chapter 4, which were (1) that fear is inimical to and the opposite of love, in general, and the Tao That is Love, in particular, and if so, then (2) attachment, founded in fear, is the supreme impediment to union with the Tao, and thus, to the recovery of our True Nature, and (3) insofar as we practice fear's opposite, love, we at once transcend fear, realize union with the Tao, and recover our True Nature.

Now, if love is the requisite remedy to the disease of fear, and hence, to attachment, then it seems reasonable to assume that Lao Tzu regards the practice of acceptance as all of a piece with the practice of love. But however reasonable this acceptance-as-love-equation may be, does Lao Tzu give us any textual reason to think that he concurs in this equation? I am convinced that he does so concur, and in support thereof consider, in the first place, the following passage:

> Because he accepts himself,
> the whole world accepts him. (Poem 30)

In this passage, Lao Tzu makes others' acceptance of us conditional on our acceptance of ourselves. On the surface, this revelation, while doubtless insightful, would seem to offer no real support for the contention that Lao Tzu identifies the practice of acceptance with the practice of love. However, on closer inspection, I believe the passage may be shown to lend strong, albeit indirect, support for this very contention. To which supportive end, recall that above I argued both the logicality and textual legitimacy (see Poem 28) of regarding acceptance as the flip side or counterpart of relinquishing control. Again, recall that, as the disposition to control is rooted in fear-based attachment (see Chapter 7), relinquishing control of ourselves necessarily entails the overcoming of fear, and therefore, the presence of fear's antithesis, love. From which recollections two corollary conclusions follow: first, when, and to the extent that, we accept ourselves, we necessarily love ourselves; and second, when, and to the extent that, we accept ourselves, we open ourselves to the love of "the whole world"—both of which corollaries we may encapsulate in the expression: As we accept/love ourselves, we deem ourselves worthy of the acceptance/love of "the whole world."

Having established the synonymy between self-acceptance and self-love, now consider two passages wherein Lao Tzu indicates the positive effects that follow from the faithful practice of self-acceptance/self-love:

> Love the world as your self;
> then you can care for all things. (Poem 13)

> Compassionate toward yourself,
> you reconcile all beings in the world. (Poem 67)

As these passages amply attest, Lao Tzu is firmly of the opinion that, as we accept/love ourselves, we can "care for" and "reconcile all beings in the world." The act of "caring" clearly denotes love, and specifically, a loving concern for others. The act of "reconciling" no less denotes love, in that to reconcile is to unite, foster harmony, effect peace—all principal, unfailing signs of love, as I have oft noted.

But if self-acceptance is equatable with self-love, and the practice of self-acceptance/self-love engenders a loving concern for others ("care for all things"), as well as unity, harmony, and peace (the "reconciliation [of] all beings in the world"), this implies that self-acceptance/self-love is the causal basis of our capacity to accept/love others. In further proof thereof I refer the Reader to our earlier discussion in this chapter wherein it was shown that selfishness, the absence of love for others, is a function of fear-based attachment. If so, then it stands well to reason that self-acceptance/self-love, indicating as it does the absence of fear, and hence of selfishness, is, as I say, the causal basis of our capacity to accept/love others. Beyond even this, however, it no less stands well to reason that self-acceptance/self-love, as the antithesis of fear, is all one with practical detachment, and is for that reason *the* means by which we not only accept/love others, but also transcend dualistically spawned fear-based attachment, and realize thereby the twofold consummate purpose of life: loving union with the Tao and the recovery our true, loving Nature. In short, when Lao Tzu writes:

> [A]ccept the world as it is . . . ,

he presupposes the prior acceptance/love of ourselves. And when he further remarks:

> If you accept the world,
> the Tao will be luminous inside you
> and you will return to your primal self., (Poem 28)

he points to self-acceptance/self-love as synonymous with practical detachment, the requisite means by which we reunite with the Tao and regain our True Nature.*

Finally, because self-acceptance/self-love, by dint of being the polar opposite of fear, and hence of selfishness, begets a loving concern for and communion with all that is, we see that Lao Tzu implicitly endorses the reciprocal relationship between the love of self and the love of others. But not only are these loves reciprocal; they are also proportional: Insofar as we love ourselves, we love others, and insofar as we love others, we love ourselves. Accordingly, the love of self and the love of others are, for Lao Tzu, both complementary and entirely commensurate forms of love. For which reason—and although self-acceptance/self-love is prior to and the cause of our capacity to accept/love others and recover our True Nature (a point I shall develop later in the chapter)—the act of acceptance may be practiced in either the self-acceptance/self-love-mode or the other-acceptance/other-love-mode. So that, in the end, acceptance of self (Poem 30) and acceptance of others (Poem 28) amount to one and the same act of acceptance, the practice of which "returns you to your primal self."

The Practice of Acceptance: Up Close and Personal

I concluded the previous section by pointing out that, notwithstanding the causal priority of self-acceptance/self-love to the acceptance/love of others, precisely because the acceptance/love of others presupposes the acceptance/love of ourselves, we may practice acceptance in either the self- or the other-acceptance-mode. This being said, the Reader may still be less than clear on what such practices *specifically* amount to. Assuming this to be the case, I shall in this section endeavor to indicate in some greater detail what acceptance does, and does not, specifically amount to.

To which specifying end, it might be well to begin by quickly dismissing one possible misconception as to the nature and practice of acceptance. I allude to the temptation to equate acceptance with resignation as the salutary means by which we overcome our attachments and regain our True Nature. That acceptance is in no way reducible to resignation is evident from the fact that, whereas hope is an integral component of acceptance (in that acceptance holds out the promise of advancing beyond our debilitating fear-condition and into a life-giving condition of freedom, spontaneity, and love), resignation betokens an out-and-out giving up on life, and so, a hopelessness with respect to life and its prospects. To be resigned to our or others' present physical, psychological, and spiritual condition is to believe that our and others' lives are fated, and hence that there is no way out of these present conditions. To lead an accepting life, by contrast, is to believe that our and others' present physical, psychological, and spiritual conditions are perfectible, and hence that there is most definitely a way out of these present conditions.

If the practice of acceptance decidedly is not at one with the practice—if we may so speak—of resignation, with what practice may we positively identify the practice of acceptance? Well, we know, as earlier stated, that the practice of acceptance is identical to the practice of love. But as valuable as this insight is, it tell us only *that* such an equation does in fact exist. Left undetermined are two all-important questions: What does the practice of acceptance/love fundamentally consist of? and, How do we go about practicing acceptance/love in our daily lives?

As to the first question, what acceptance/love fundamentally consists of? I think all would agree that love, in its truest and deepest sense, is *unconditional* love, namely, the sort of love that gives without expecting a return or demanding that someone look or behave in a certain, preordained or prescribed way.

If we can agree that this is what love fundamentally consists of, then acceptance, to be truly synonymous with this expression of love, must carry a like unconditionally loving significance. Accordingly, I propose that acceptance, rightly nuanced as a mode of unconditional love, essentially amounts to *the non-judgmental reception of others and ourselves in whatever fear-state we or they may happen to be*. Or as Lao Tzu obliquely puts it:

> The Master is available to all people
> and doesn't reject anyone [including herself.] (Poem 27)

Either this, or (1) we judge ourselves and others, in which case we fail to receive and so to love ourselves and others, or (2) we accept ourselves and others conditionally, in which case we receive and love ourselves and others conditionally. Whence, my view that acceptance as an expression of unconditional love is all of a piece with an attitude of non-judgment. Which brings us to our second question: How do we practice acceptance/love—defined, as we have just seen, as an attitude of non-judgment—in our daily lives? In the balance of this section, I shall respond to this question, first, as it has a bearing on our acceptance/love of others, and afterwards, on our acceptance/love of ourselves.

Acceptance of Others

As was just noted, we non-judgmentally receive others when we accept them in their various fear-states. In more exact terms, to so receive others means that we accept them despite and in the face of their non-loving moods, habits, beliefs, actions, and so on. I say "non-loving moods, etc.," because, as we noticed especially in Chapters 4, 5, and 6, as we abide in attachment, in fear-based desire, we inhibit our naturally loving Nature. This inhibition begets the three primary classes of affliction, confusion, sorrow, and a waning of inner peace. Which afflictions more specifically translate to such dour, personally experienced states as desperation, frustration, restlessness, jealousy, anger, depression, anxiety, and despair, not to mention feelings of inadequacy and unworthiness. With respect to our posture toward others, these three classes of affliction include extremes of selfishness, a need to control, and an "I-other" mentality that all-too easily leads to, and even justifies on moral, religious, and legal grounds, the abuse of others.

In brief, we non-judgmentally receive others in their sundry fear-states when we accept them, for example, as angry, selfish, anxious, controlling, prejudiced, addicted, or even as sadistic, cruel, or murderous! Which is not to say, be it well-noted, that when we so accept others we necessarily agree with or condone their views and/or actions. As a matter of fact, we may be vehemently opposed to their views and/or actions. To accept others means only that we *non-judgmentally receive them despite their views and/or actions, that we refrain from judging them intrinsically evil*, even when we may be convinced that their views and/or actions are intrinsically evil. Moreover, from the perspective of the *Tao Te Ching*, there are at least two outstanding reasons to desist from judging others. For if, as this spiritual classic teaches, our True Nature is an immanent expression of the Tao, and for that reason, naturally loving, then to judge others to be inherently evil is both a false judgment (reason one) and a judgment against, a rejection of, the Tao Itself (reason two)!

Allowing, then, that to truly accept others is to non-judgmentally receive them, exactly how does this act of acceptance assist others in overcoming their attachments, and thereby, recovering their True Nature? The answer rests on the premise that, as acceptance, fundamentally regarded, *is* unconditional love, to accept others is to offer them a gift of unconditional love. Should they choose to accept this gift—why they might not I shall discuss shortly—they add, as it were, to their stock of available love-energy. And, because love is the antidote to fear, in accepting our gift, they thereby enhance their capacity and resolve to liberate themselves from their various attachment-spawned fear-states. (What this practically amounts to is an experientially verifiable test to the effect that, when you allow others to so accept you, you will almost certainly find that your besetting fear-state(s), say, your anxiety and depression, will be, if not completely healed—which just might happen!—at least much alleviated. In other words, I would lay odds that you will emerge from this accepting experience feeling freer, less fearful, and more peaceful, as you, at the same time, gain a new, less forbidding, and more hopeful outlook on your fear-induced problems, quite apart from anything your accepting friend may say or do for you. But don't take my word for it. Taste and see for yourself whether allowing others to accept you is the healing, liberating, and spiritual boon Lao Tzu believes it to be.)

Two remarks made in the preceding paragraph require an explanatory word or two. The first concerns my statement that, when we allow others to accept us, we "add to our stock of available love-energy." An obvious implication here is that, prior to others' loving acceptance of us, we possess what I have dubbed "love-energy," with the related implication that our "love-energy" is not entirely a function of others' loving acceptance. What justifies these implications, as far as the *Tao Te Ching* is concerned, is in fact its view that our True Nature is naturally loving. For if so, then it stands well to reason that we are already possessed of "love-energy," and that, so possessed, we aren't always and necessarily beholden to others' loving acceptance to overcome our fears and act in a loving manner. Finally, it no less stands well to reason that, as our Nature is naturally loving, our fears, be they ever so many, can never completely vanquish our loving Nature. The moral of which unvanquishing of our True Nature is that we always possess the naturally loving capacity, weakened though it may be by our contagion of fears, to transcend our fear-states, recover our True Nature, and act in a naturally loving manner.

Self-Acceptance

Which brings us to the second remark from two paragraphs ago in need of clarification, to wit, that we may elect to decline others' gift of love to us. Whatever would induce us to reject so priceless a gift? The answer is that we ultimately reject others' love because we are lacking in the second mode of acceptance, *self* acceptance. To better appreciate the significance of this "lacking," we need only recall that self-acceptance is the selfsame as self-love. For which reason we may substitute self-love for self-acceptance and change the answer to read: we reject others' gift of acceptance because we are deficient in self-love. In other words, the reason we reject others' gift of love is that we deem ourselves unworthy of their gift. Which is only to say that, in the final analysis, we reject others' love because we have first rejected ourselves!

The spiritual law here is that we get what we are prepared to accept, no more, no less. And such acceptance is predicated on how well we accept/love ourselves. Which means not only that self-acceptance is a way back to our True Nature, as was earlier noted, but that self-acceptance actually takes causal precedence over the acceptance of others in recovering our True Nature, and for two main reasons. In the first place, and as was just seen, if we can't accept/love ourselves, neither can we accept others' acceptance/love.[8] In the second place, if we can't accept/love ourselves, neither can we accept/love others, a view Lao Tzu expresses in more positive terms in these erst-cited passages:

> Love the world as your self;
> then you can care for all things. (Poem 13)
>
> Compassionate toward yourself,
> you reconcile all beings in the world. (Poem 67)

Then again, and to state an earlier point somewhat differently, Lao Tzu also, even if more obliquely, suggests that self-acceptance/self-love is the necessary precondition to accepting/loving others when, in another previously cited Poem, he remarks that, if we can accept/love others ("the world"), "the Tao will be luminous inside us and we will return to our primal self." (Poem 28) In light of Poems 13 and 67, which clearly affirm that our capacity to love others is a function of our capacity to love ourselves, we see that presupposed in Poem 28, whereby we are urged to accept/love others as the condition of having the Tao "luminous inside us and returning to our primal self," is the prior acceptance/love of ourselves.

One important consequence of the above is that, while it is perfectly true to hold that the practice of acceptance *is* practical detachment, and thus that acceptance is the way out of our attachment-begotten fear-states, given self-acceptance's causally precedent position over the acceptance of others, in the interest of accuracy, we might amend the acceptance/practical detachment equation as follows: The acceptance of others is practical detachment, *remotely taken;* self-acceptance is practical detachment, *proximately taken*.

It would seem, then, that, as told by the *Tao Te Ching*, our paramount task in life is to accept ourselves, for only then can we accept others, reconnect with the Tao, and recover our True Nature. So how do we go about accepting ourselves? And here the answer is, just as we accept others by non-judgmentally receiving them in whatever fear-state we may happen to find them, so we accept ourselves by non-judgmentally receiving ourselves in whatever fear-state we may happen to find ourselves. And this concretely means, as we saw when it comes to accepting others, that we accept ourselves, for example, as envious, confused, physically incapacitated, addicted, depressed, anxious, controlling, vengeful, and so on. It means, that is to say, not that we regard such fear-states as acceptable, but rather that we refrain from judging ourselves inherently evil because we harbor such fear-states. It means, in short—and this is a point often missed when we are enjoined to "judge not"—that we have as much of an obligation not to judge ourselves, in view of our Tao-born naturally loving Nature, as we have not to judge others, in view of their Tao-born naturally loving Nature.

Furthermore, and to develop a point first broached when discussing the acceptance of others, that we can accept ourselves is guaranteed by our naturally loving Nature. For given our naturally loving Nature, we possess both the capacity and the motivation to accept ourselves, notwithstanding the length, breadth, and depth of our fear-beset condition. Not that our fears don't impede our capacity and determination to accept ourselves. As love's polar opposite, fear inhibits "our stock of available love-energy," which means that, the more fearful we are, the less appreciative we will be of our naturally loving Nature, with the result that it becomes all the more difficult to accept/love ourselves. Still, precisely because our Nature is *naturally* loving, fear can never obliterate our True Nature, as, I believe, the following line of reasoning succinctly demonstrates. Fear, as love's opposite, runs contrary to our True Nature. Our True Nature is an immanent expression of the Eternal Tao That is Love Itself. Therefore, to assert that fear can extinguish our True Nature is to assert the flat contradiction that fear can extinguish the Eternal Tao That is Love Itself.

Finally, before concluding this section, and lest I be misunderstood when I state that we possess the naturally loving capacity to surmount our fear-states and act in a naturally loving manner, please note that I am in no way denying the healing efficacy of others' acceptance of us when it comes to overcoming our fear-states. As noted above, when we allow others to accept us, this only enhances our capacity and resolve to conquer our fear-states. In so doing, we add the love offered to us by others to our own "stock of available love-energy," thereby increasing the amount of "usable" love-energy, and hence, our potential for healing, physically, psychologically, and spiritually.

At the same time, neither am I denying that, especially in the early stages of our lives, others' acceptance of us plays a critical role in our development physically, psychologically, and spiritually. Again, I am not denying that it is usually a lot easier and typically a good deal more enjoyable to work at healing ourselves when we are supported by loving, accepting others. Yet again, I am not denying that, more often than not, most of us require others' loving assistance as catalysts to, if not actually essential to, our healing. Nor am I even denying that some, perhaps most, of us will always require others' loving assistance if we are to summon the courage and motivation to work at healing ourselves of our various fear-states. In sum, I am in no way denying the significance and, at times, indispensability, of others' loving acceptance when it comes to healing ourselves.

But to admit all this is not, I repeat, to admit the absolute necessity of others' acceptance in the healing process. The heart and soul of healing is, and will always remain, self-acceptance, without which others' acceptance, be it ever so loving, will avail us for nought. Stated more technically, we might say that others' acceptance is the potent *occasion* of healing, self-acceptance is the true *cause of* healing. That is, others' acceptance creates a favorable, love-enriched environment, so to speak, wherein healing is greatly facilitated. Self-acceptance, however, is the actual cause of healing, in that, save for self-acceptance, not only will we reject others' loving energy toward healing our fear-states; we will also reject *our own* loving energy toward healing our fear-states. Which means, in the final rendering, that, if we can accept ourselves, we will doubtless gladly and gratefully accept others' loving assistance in our healing behalf, but that, should others' assistance herein not be forthcoming, we will still possess the self-loving wherewithal to heal ourselves, by ourselves.[9]

For Lao Tzu, then, nature's supreme gift to us is its positive lesson for reuniting with the Tao and recovering our True Nature, the practice of acceptance, and in particular, the practice of self-acceptance. It only remains for us to consider what life is like for one who, through the faithful practice of self-acceptance, has mastered attachment and realized the pinnacle of spiritual success, the "Tao luminous inside him" and the "return to his primal self." To this extraordinary individual I shall devote the final chapter of this book.

Notes

1. Cited in *A Source Book in Indian Philosophy*. Edited by S. Radhakrishnan and Charles A. Moore (Princeton, N.J.: Princeton University Press, 1957), p. 50.

2. Cited in *Breakthrough: Meister Eckhart's Creation Spirituality in New Translation*. Introduction and Commentaries by Matthew Fox, O.P. (Garden City, NY: Image Books, 1980), Sermon Fifteen, p. 214.

3. Cited by Aldous Huxley, *The Perennial Philosophy* (New York: Harper Colophon Books, 1945) p. 87. For an excellent discussion of detachment's pivotal place in both Eastern and Western spiritual traditions, see *Ibid.*, pp. 96–125.

4. *Ibid.*, p. 219.

5. Cited in *A Source Book in Indian Philosophy*, p. 72.

6. *Ibid.*, p. 87.

7. *The Yoga Sutras of Patanjali*. Translation and Commentary by Sri Swami Satchidananda (Yogaville, Virginia: Integral Yoga Publications, 1978), pp. 24–25.

8. The important point here is that others can't practice detachment in the sense of self-acceptance/self-love *for us*. If we are to recover our True Nature, we can only do so if we, and we alone, are prepared to accept ourselves, to non-judgmentally receive ourselves, despite the presence of our dualistically born, fear-based attached states. In other words, what

Lao Tzu is asserting, in contrast to most Western religions, is that belief in an external or vicarious savior as necessary for our salvation is a dangerous illusion.

9. For a fuller, more in-depth discussion of self-love/self-acceptance *vis-à-vis* physical, psychological, and spiritual wholeness, happiness, and liberation, see Joseph A. Magno, *Self-Love: The Heart of Healing* (Lanham, Maryland: University Press of America, 2000).

CHAPTER NINE

Conclusion: Our True Self Regained

> The Master keeps her mind
> always at one with the Tao;
> that is what gives her her radiance.
>
> *Lao Tzu, Tao Te Ching, Poem 21*

Introduction

In Chapter 8, we saw that primarily through the practice of self-acceptance (alias practical detachment) the Master at once recovers her True Nature and reunites with the Tao. We have also seen, here and there, and usually in a piecemeal manner, certain positive effects the Master's recovery and reconnection herein have on her as well as others. It is probably safe to assume that the Reader hasn't bothered to piece together into a coherent whole all these various, disjointed effects resulting from the Master's recovery and reconnection. If this is a fairly safe assumption, then, as these effects collectively represent the culmination of spiritual success as told by the *Tao Te Ching*, it is only fitting that I conclude this opus with a summation of (1) the main attributes that serve to identify the Master and (2) the Master's influence on other human beings, in particular, and the non-human world, in general.

Attributes of the Master

As to the Master herself, consider, for starters, the final two lines from Poem 22:

> Only in being lived by the Tao
> can you be truly yourself.[1]

The Master, and the Master alone, is "truly herself." And why? Because she alone is "lived by the Tao." Here, Lao Tzu alludes to one of the major, recurring themes of the *Tao Te Ching*, that our "True Nature," the Nature that, due to the Tao's willful "Fall" most have "forgotten," is an immanent expression of the Tao. So that, "to be lived by Tao" means that the Master, having recovered/remembered her True Nature, *is* the Tao expressing Itself immanently in and through the Master!

Next, let's take a look at some of the principal ways in which the Master, who is "being lived by the Tao," acquits herself in life. Two poems are especially revealing in this regard. Thus, in the first stanza of Poem 35, Lao Tzu declares that,

> She who is centered in the Tao
> can go where she wishes, without danger.
> She perceives the universal harmony,
> even amid great pain,
> because she has found peace in her heart.

In this stanza, the Reader will recognize several marks of the Master heretofore noted. The Master ("She who is centered in the Tao") lives in freedom ("can go where she wishes"), because she has overcome the main obstacle to freedom, attachment-begotten fear ("without danger.") Fear, implying as it does an "I-other" dichotomous take on reality, is mainly responsible for the tendency to regard others as "unknown," and so as "different," and so as "dangerous," and so as "others to be feared." Caught in fear's intractable web, and viewing life as "dangerous," we naturally become more cautious in our day-to-day doings, with the result that our freedom, both in the sense of our freedom to choose (our free will) and our freedom to choose among available options, is significantly curtailed.

At the same time, this stanza alludes to another notable mark of the Master, what we might term in the present context her 'intuitive savvy'. Centered in the Tao, the Master is intuitively in tune with the Tao, which means that, in this case, she is insightfully aware of whether a given situation conduces to her well-being, physically, psychologically, and spiritually. So that, not only is the Master free to go where she pleases; guided by her 'intuitive savvy', she is also aware of whether where she freely goes will redound to her physical, psychological, and spiritual benefit.[2]

Finally, the Master, shorn of fear, and centered in the Tao, possesses a love-born unified consciousness ("she perceives the universal harmony.") As such, she knows in her heart that all is well, "even amid great pain," because, being at one with all things by virtue of her oneness with the Tao That is Love, she possesses the peace that passeth understanding ("she has found peace in her heart.")

Another poem even more revelatory of the ways in which the Master conducts herself in her daily life is Poem 16, which begins by reminding us that,

> Each separate being in the universe
> returns to the common source.

In Chapter 4, I referred to this promissory message as the "Good News of the *Tao Te Ching*." The Master, accordingly, is a person who, insofar as it is possible on this plane of existence, has "returned to the common source [the Tao]." Next, we are further reminded that

> Returning to the source is serenity.*

---

* In Poem 14, Lao Tzu also states: "Just realize where you come from: this is the essence of wisdom." That is, communion with the Tao begets both love-born serenity (peace) and wisdom, the intuitive ability to know and do the loving thing in a specific situation.

and conversely that,

> If you don't realize the source,
> you stumble in confusion and sorrow.

All this—the serenity (peace) that is the experience and sign of reunion with the Tao, the confusion and sorrow that are the twin experiences and signs of disunion from the Tao—we have abundantly examined in the foregoing chapters. Suffice it to say, as far as the Master is concerned, that as one who abounds in peace (that passeth understanding), she is largely, if not entirely, immune to attachment's primary ill-begotten progeny, confusion and sorrow.

Otherwise stated, the Master is the enlightened one, the one who "realizes," who has awakened to, "where she comes from." And, to

> realize where you come from,

is to begin to exhibit certain 'enlightened' dispositions and behavioral traits, which Lao Tzu delineates as follows:

> you naturally become tolerant,
> disinterested, amused,
> kindhearted as a grandmother,
> dignified as a king.
> Immersed in the wonder of the Tao,
> you can go where life brings you,
> and when death comes, you are ready.

I shall comment upon each of these traits in turn, beginning with,

"The Master naturally becomes tolerant..."

In other words, the Master becomes naturally accepting of herself and others. And this because, in "realizing where she comes from," the Master has regained her true, naturally loving Nature, so that self-acceptance and the acceptance of others, as modes of unconditional love, become, for the Master, co-natural responses to herself and others.*

"The Master naturally becomes disinterested..."

"Disinterested," in the present context, and as used by certain Western spiritual writers,[3] signifies detachment, and specifically, 'ideal detachment' in contrast to 'practical detachment.' Practical detachment, we recall, amounts to acceptance of ourselves in whatever fear-state we may happen to find ourselves, e.g., as jealous, spiteful, guilt-ridden, and so on. The Master, having regained her true, naturally loving Nature by dint of her reidentification with the Tao That is Love, is thus not subject to attachment-born fear-states. For this reason, her desire for a given outcome is neither beset with fear as to the realization of the outcome nor, should she realize the desired outcome, ridden with the fear that her realized outcome will be short-lived. In other words, the Master's detachment is disinterested, not in the sense that the Master is utterly indifferent to outcomes (in which case the Master would lack the desire or motivation to pursue even spiritually self-enriching goals or outcomes), but rather in the sense that, freed of such fear-modes as the need to control the outcome, as well as bias, worry, doubt, and anxiety as to the realization of a desired outcome, she is able to "do her job, then let go" of the outcome (Poem 24).

* As discussed in Chapter 8, all individuals, by dint of their naturally loving Tao-Nature, possess the natural *capacity* to practice self- and other-acceptance, although they may fail to do so due to their attachment-born fears. The Master, by contrast, not only possesses the natural capacity to practice self- and other-acceptance; beyond this, she is someone who, by dint of her recovery of her naturally lovng Nature, effortlessly, spontaneously, and unfailingly, in short, naturally *actualizes* that capacity.

"The Master naturally becomes amused…"

This attribute is reminiscent of those depictions of the Buddha with an ever-so subtle smile on his face! And why is the Buddha smiling ever-so subtly? A common answer is that the Buddha smiles because he knows that, appearances notwithstanding, all is as it should be, all is and will be well, which knowledge, being pleasing to the Buddha, accounts for his grin. But this gives rise to an even more basic question: What convinces the Buddha that all is well? And the more basic answer is that the Buddha is ultimately so convinced because, having transcended the dualistic illusion, he has thereby transcended fear And because fear is the chief inhibitor of mirth (as in it is difficult to find much to smile about, much less laugh about, when we're immersed in our fear-based problems), and the Buddha has mastered fear, the Buddha, like the Taoist Master, is free to smile, to find life "amusing." The moral of which story is that the spiritual Master, perhaps more than anyone else, can appreciate a good joke when she hears one!

"The Master naturally becomes kindhearted as a grandmother…"

Anyone who has had an agreeable grandmotherly experience cannot but appreciate what Lao Tzu wishes to convey here. The term "grandmother," assuming that *your* grandmother is or was truly "kindhearted," naturally evokes such pleasantly safe sentiments as security, stability, and warmth, as well as such noble character traits as generosity, compassion, sympathy, patience, benevolence, and hospitality. That Lao Tzu elects to compare the Master to a "kindhearted grandmother" means that he ascribes to the Master similar 'grandmotherly' qualities. Is this comparison warranted? I suggest that it is entirely warranted. After all, in whose presence are we more apt to feel warmly safe and secure than in the presence of a person who lives life worry-free, offers us unconditional (non-judgmental) acceptance, and exudes a profoundly tangible and unextinguishable peace? Again, who is more apt to manifest such altruistic character traits as generosity, compassion, sympathy, patience, benevolence, and hospitality than this same fearless, unconditionally accepting, and peace-filled person? In short, who is more suited to don the title of "kindhearted grandmother!" than the Master, the one who, because "she has realized where she comes from," has regained her naturally loving Nature?

"The Master is dignified as a king."

There is, of course, an obvious sense in which this designation is supremely applicable to the Master. When we review the attributes that collectively distinguish the Master—her freedom, fearlessness, intuitive savvy as to what is the most beneficial and pleasing course of action, unified consciousness, imperturbable inner peace, unconditional acceptance of herself and others, ideal detachment, sense of humor, and her ensemble of "kindhearted grandmotherly" qualities, all of which are consequent upon the recovery of her naturally loving Nature, and so of "being lived by the Tao"—"dignified as a king" is evidently more than justified as a depiction of the Master.

Another fairly obvious sense in which "dignified as a king" eminently befits the Master recalls our discussion in Chapter 6 of the true leader. For if the term "king" denotes a leader, and a *true* leader, in Lao Tzu's estimation, is someone who is detachedly at the service of people, as well as intuitively attuned to their needs, mentality, tastes, and mood (see Poems 66 and 68), then who is more deserving of the title, "dignified as a king," than the Master? Not that the Master is likely to be an actual king or ruler. Indeed, because

> The Master's constant practice is humility.
> He doesn't glitter like a jewel
> but lets himself be shaped by the Tao,
> as rugged and common as stone. (Poem 39)

What is more, the Master knows full well that since all beings are expressions of the Tao (see Poem 51), she

> ... doesn't think that she is better
> than anyone else. (Poem 77)

Nor does the Master even aspire to be an actual king or ruler.

> The Master doesn't try to be powerful ... (Poem 38)

and

> ... never reaches for the great ... (Poem 63)

Ultimately, the only crown, you might say, the Master aspires to is the Tao:

> The Master cares about nothing but the Tao.

Which is precisely why

> ... the Master can care for all things. (Poem 64)

And so it is that

> The Master is content to serve by example
> and not to impose her will.
> She is pointed, but doesn't pierce.
> Straightforward, but supple. (Poem 58)

If anything, then, the Master is content to lead by example, and in so doing, to

> ... simply remind people
> of who they have always been. (Poem 64)

Because the Master is beyond the need to control others and events, like the Tao, Who "nourishes by not forcing" (Poem 81), she is beyond the need to lead by force. Which is not to say that the Master is loathe to express her point of view ("She is pointed...") Bereft of fear, and guided by her intuitive savvy, she will

> ... express herself completely,
> then keep quiet. (Poem 23)

And this "Because she believes in herself," and so, neither "tries to convince others" nor "needs others' approval." (Poem 30) ("She is pointed, but doesn't pierce.")

Again, though "The Master sees things as they are," she "doesn't try to control them," but "lets things go their own way." (Poem 29) ("Straightforward, but supple.")

Yet again, and even more importantly, the Master realizes that most individuals rely primarily on conceptually based modes of knowing (see Chapters 1,2 and 5), and that as long as they do, they "will never grasp her teachings," much less be able to put them into practice. The Master realizes, in other words, the futility and downright foolishness of attempting to convince others of truths accessible only to the clear light of intuitive vision ("If you want to know me [and hence my teachings], look inside your heart.") (Poem 70)[4] For all these reasons, then—for her ensemble of noble qualities, in general, and her leadership qualities, in particular—who more than the Master deserves the appellation "dignified as a king"?

Finally, of the Master, Lao Tzu writes:

"Immersed in the wonder of the Tao,
she can go where life brings her,
and when death comes, she is ready."

It is often said that the most formidable of fears is the fear of dying,[5] and that if we can but conquer this fear, what (less formidable) fear can't we conquer? In this verse, Lao Tzu highlights the Master's fearlessness by stating that, "immersed in the wonder of the Tao"s loving embrace, even the greatest of all fears, the fear of death, holds no sway over the Master. Having defeated this fear, the Master enjoys maximal freedom to go with the flow of events, whether pleasant or unpleasant, and in general, to accept herself, others, and events unshackled by fear-based reservations ("she can go where life brings her…")

Moreover, and as Lao Tzu remarks in Poem 74,

> If you aren't afraid of dying,
> there is nothing you can't achieve.

Not only is the Master, who "isn't afraid of dying," free to go with the flow of life; she is also free to pursue her personal goals unencumbered by debilitating fears as to her ability to achieve her goals, worthiness to receive her goals, or whether, upon realizing her goals, she is fated to lose them.

Then too, states Lao Tzu, the Master, who "isn't afraid of dying," lives a life of perfect detachment ("she has nothing left to hold on to…") Because she is perfectly detached, and so beyond a fear-based, illusory disunified consciousness, she is beyond the primal affliction, "confusion" ("she has no illusions in her mind…") Again, because she is perfectly detached, and so immune to attachment-born, fear-based suffering, she is beyond the second primal affliction, "sorrow" ("she has no resistance in her body…") Yet again, because she is perfectly detached, and so possesses a love-based, unified consciousness, the Master, "immersed in the wonder of the Tao," isn't bound by conceptual modes of knowing ("She doesn't think about her actions…"), but is intuitively aware of and able to carry out the most appropriate and loving course of action in a given situation ("her actions flow from the core of her being.") (Poem 50)

Finally, the ultimate prize the Master, who "embraces death with her whole heart," gains is the conviction that "she will endure forever." (Poem 33) In other words, the Master gains nothing less than the inner certainty that death is not the end of her but merely a stage on her True Nature's way. She gains, that is to say, the greatest of all realizations, that she, as an immanent expression of the eternal Tao, is herself an *immortal* expression of the eternal Tao!

In short, the imperturbably peaceful, fearless, entirely free, thoroughly accepting, fully detached, optimally intuitive, confusion- and sorrow-transcending, immortal Master is, for Lao Tzu, nothing less than humankind's exemplar par excellence, the perfectly fulfilled and Self-realized human being ("She holds nothing back from life ..."). For all of which reasons, the Master, far from fearing death, is more than

... ready for death,
as a man is ready for sleep
after a good day's work. (Poem 50)

Such, then, are the principal attributes that characterize Lao Tzu's ideal person, the Master. But as noted at the commencement of this chapter, the Master is also identifiable by her influence on other human and non-human beings. Accordingly, the balance of this chapter, and thus of this book, I shall devote to the how, the what, and the why of the Master's influence on human and non-human beings alike.

The Master's "Cosmic" Influence

The Master, as we have seen, serves others both by example and by her acceptance of them: by example, through her ensemble of Masterly attributes, through her modeling for others a perfectly fulfilled and Self-realized life, through her demonstrating to others the way to realize a perfectly fulfilled and Self-realized life, and through her inspiring others to pursue for themselves a perfectly fulfilled and Self-realized life; by acceptance, through her non-judgmental, unconditionally loving reception of them in whatever attachment-begotten fear-state she may find them, thereby greatly assisting others in accepting themselves, overcoming their fear-states, and achieving in their own right perfect fulfillment and Self-realization.

But there exists an even more cosmic way in which the Master serves others, and indeed, the entire natural order. To appreciate this "more cosmic way," recall a point first broached in Chapter 2, namely, that all beings, be they "great" or "small," *are* the Tao immanently

Self-manifesting Itself (on this plane) in space and time. In view of the Tao's immanence in and as all beings, it plainly follows that all beings, be they "great" or "small," are essentially interconnected.[6] From which it further follows that all beings, to a greater or lesser extent, exert an influence on one another, that what happens to one, happens, in some measure, to all.

To employ a rough analogy, it is as if each of us is a cell in a vast organism. A healthy cell irradiates positive energy, an unhealthy cell negative energy, to all other cells, and hence to the organism as a whole. Moreover, if enough cells irradiate positive energy to the other cells, it creates a critical mass that has the effect of raising the energy level of the less healthy cells, thereby increasing the health of the organism as a whole. Conversely, if enough cell irradiate negative energy to the other cells, it creates a critical mass that has the effect of lowering the energy level of the more healthy cells, thereby decreasing the health of the organism as a whole. The point, then, is that, as John Donne poetically articulates it, "No man is an island," that in a way that boggles understanding, for better or worse, we are all in this thing called existence together.

Which is precisely why the Master is so critical to the health and well-being of her fellow humans, in particular, and the natural order, in general. The Master, by virtue of her reidentification with the Tao, and consequent recovery of her true, loving Nature, naturally irradiates to all creatures the most potent of all energies, the energy of love. What is more, because the Master is "lived by the Tao," and the Tao is Love Itself, she naturally irradiates a love-energy that is immeasurably life-enhancing, physically, mentally, emotionally, and spiritually. Finally, the Master irradiates love-energy simply by being her "radiant" self, and quite apart from any specific work she performs in the service of her fellow creatures. Indeed, even were the Master to do nothing in particular, choosing instead to live a life of solitude, she would nevertheless

> ... make use of her solitude,
> embracing her aloneness, realizing
> that she is one with the whole universe. (Poem 42)

In brief, on this mortal coil, at least, there exists no more significant, necessary, and powerful world benefactor than the Master, whose heart and mind is "always at one with the Tao." (Poem 21)

The Master's Cosmic Influence on the Natural Order

Let's now look at various poems in which Lao Tzu expressly indicates how the Master benefits the natural order. Were we to succinctly state the principal way in which the Master serves the world we could do no better, I believe, than to designate the Master the 'supreme agent of world harmony'. And nowhere does Lao Tzu more plainly say as much than when he writes:

> If powerful men and women
> could remain centered in the Tao,
> all things would be in harmony. (Poem 32)

We might paraphrase this passage as follows: "If a sufficient number of Masters could remain centered in the Tao," if, that is, there were a critical mass of love-energy, then "all things would be in harmony." As noted in previous chapters, harmony, synonymous with union, communion, accord, concord, balance, and so on, is one of the principal effects of love. Accordingly, Masters, by virtue of their oneness with the Tao That is Love, in an unparalleled way irradiate a love-energy to the world such that, were it to achieve a critical mass, it would be productive of universal harmony.

Or, we might state the Master's influence on the world in this way: the Master, by virtue of her unsurpassed love-energy, effects harmony by reconciling the Tao's 'Primal Conceptual Design' or "Pattern' for Creation, Its Yin and Yang co-principles. As we learned in Chapter 3, Yin, roughly translatable as 'Feminine,' and Yang, roughly translatable as 'Masculine,' are the Tao's primally conceived, all-encompassing constitutive co-principles and models for all creation. In other words, for Taoism, all things, be they male (Yang) or female (Yin), are yet fundamentally and complementarily composed of *both* Yin and Yang principles, much like the negative and positive poles of an electric current (another way of depicting Yin and Yang principles, respectively.) As such, the final goal of all things, in keeping with the Tao's Primal Design, may be viewed in terms of striking the delicate balance between these co-principles as the way to realizing happiness, wholeness, and liberation. And since it is love, and in particular, loving communion with the Tao, that effects a balanced, harmonious existence, it becomes apparent that the way we ultimately reconcile the Yin/Yang poles of our Nature, and so realize happiness, wholeness, and liberation, is, first and foremost, through the practice of love.

Which is where the Master, before all else, enters the cosmic picture. For the Master, at one with the Tao That is Love,

> Knows the white,
> yet keeps to the black;

that is, embodies the delicate balance between the Yin (black) and Yang (white) co-principles of her Nature. For this reason, the Master is

> ... a pattern for the world. [And]
> If you are a pattern for the world,
> The Tao will be strong inside you
> and there will be nothing you can't do. (Poem 28)

With the "Tao ... strong inside her," one thing the Master is eminently equipped to do, even without trying, is to transmit to the world a love-energy that can accelerate others' efforts to balance the Yin/Yang poles of their Nature, thereby greatly facilitating the goal of personal and universal harmony. Which is only to say that,

> When male [Yang] and female [Yin] combine,
> all things achieve harmony. (Poem. 42)

Lao Tzu specifically refers to the Master's harmonizing influence on nature writ large in such passages as the following:

If powerful men and women
could center themselves in the Tao,
the whole world would be transformed
by itself, in its natural rhythms. (Poem 37)

In harmony with the Tao,
the sky is clear and spacious,
the earth is solid and full,
all creatures flourish together,
content with the way they are,
endlessly repeating themselves,
endlessly renewed.

On the other hand,

When man interferes with the Tao,
the sky becomes filthy,
the earth becomes depleted,
the equilibrium crumbles,
creatures become extinct. (Poem 39)

These passages, I believe, are self-explanatory, save that I would just comment that rarely in spiritual literature has the link between human beings and the state of the natural order been more in evidence than in the *Tao Te Ching*. Above, I referred to the divine interconnectedness of all reality. Here, we see in bold relief Lao Tzu's acknowledgement of that interconnectedness, and the consequent responsibility we humans bear for the condition of the world. In other words, for Lao Tzu, nothing happens "by chance." Such phenomena as earthquakes, volcanic eruptions, plagues, disease, famines, and draughts, usually styled "acts of God" and/or "natural disasters," as well as such obviously man-made unwholesome conditions as pollution, depleted natural resources, and the untimely extinction of various vegetative and animal species, are in actuality, contends Lao Tzu, directly related to and reflective of the level of disharmony wrought by humankind's dearth of love due to its disconnection from the Tao That is Love. Apparently, Lao Tzu, in agreement with the Mahayana tradition of Buddhism, is interestingly of the opinion that no one is fully liberated until the whole of creation is fully liberated!

The Master's Cosmic Influence on Human Beings

As to the Master's harmonizing influence on human beings as such, Lao Tzu writes that, if only enough men and women could center themselves in the Tao,

> People would be content
> with their simple, everyday lives,
> in harmony, and free of desire.
>
> Where there is no desire,
> all things are at peace. (Poem 37)

If enough men and women return to the Tao, people will experience ideal detachment ("free from desire"). As such, they will live their everyday lives unburdened by fear-based doubts and concerns ("People would be content ...") and in love-born communion with one another ("in harmony ...") Ultimately, because they have transcended the dualistic illusion, and so, its prime effect, fear, they will live unceasingly in loving communion with the Tao Itself, a communion the infallible sign of which is peace ("Where there is no desire, all things are at peace.")

Or, as Lao Tzu more succinctly puts the Master's harmonizing influence on humankind, if enough men and women could center themselves in the Tao,

> The world would become a paradise.
> All people would be at peace,
> and the law would be written in their hearts. (Poem 32)

So conceived by Lao Tzu, paradise will be realized when a sufficient number of men and women become Masters, that is, (1) live in loving communion with the Tao, the infallible sign of which is peace ("All people will be at peace ...) and, precisely because of their loving communion, (2) have largely transcended conceptual knowing in favor of intuitive knowing, whereby they directly and immediately perceive the most lovingly appropriate course of action in a given situation ("and the law would be written in their hearts.")[7]

In the final analysis, all that has been heretofore said as to the Master's harmonizing influence on her fellow human beings may be summarily put as follows: She, more than anyone else, through her Tao-like bequest of love, assists others in "becoming genuine." (Poem 54) By this simple phrase, Lao Tzu reminds us that our paramount goal in life is to remember the ineffably glorious truth that who we truly are, our True Nature, is the Tao immanently expressing Itself in and through each and everyone of us. Not that the Master's love can make or cause us to remember our True Nature, a point Lao Tzu alludes to when he remarks:

> How do I know this is true?
> By looking inside myself. (Poem 54)

As discussed in Chapter 8, the love/acceptance others bestow upon us acts as an invaluable occasion, a potent energy-source, that greatly facilitates our capacity to heal ourselves of our various attachment-spawned fear-states. The actual cause of such healing is our Nature's naturally loving capacity to accept/love ourselves (practical detachment), which is to say, to non-judgmentally receive ourselves in whatever attachment-induced fear-state we may find ourselves, be it as guilt-ridden, controlling, envious, depressed, or what have you. Because love is the antidote to fear, as we accept/love ourselves, we gradually release ourselves of the fears that impede our reconnection to the Tao, and thus, the recovery/remembrance of our True Nature.

And yet, if the Master's gift of love can't of itself cause us to recollect our True Nature, and if the responsibility herein rests, ultimately, upon our own free decision to accept/love ourselves, fears and all, as the "cosmic" benefactor of the natural order and the human race, par excellence, it is no exaggeration to state that, were it not for the Master, the "paradise" Lao Tzu envisions, and indeed, prophecies (see Poem 16), would be no more than an impossible dream. That we can dare to dream this dream is, when all is said and done, the Master's greatest boon to the world, the proof, if you will, that where the Master is, so can we be.

Notes

1. Compare St. Paul's "I live now not with my own life but with the life of Christ who lives in me." (Galatians: 2:20, The Jerusalem Bible), and the Buddha's "Self has disappeared and the truth has taken its abode in me." Cited by Paul Carus, *The Gospel of Buddha* (LaSalle, IL: Open Court, 1894), p. 160.

2. Speaking of intuitive savvy in an ideal sense, Lao Tzu writes: "Center your country in the Tao and evil will have no power. Not that it isn't there, but you'll be able to step out of its way." (Poem 60)

3. See, for example, Aldous Huxley's superb compendium of spirituality, East and West, *The Perennial Philosophy* (New York: Harper Colophon Books, 1944), pp. 81, 83, 92. In a similar manner, and as Huxley points out, St. Francois de Sales was fond of referring to detachment as "holy indifference." See *Ibid.*, p.98–99.

4. In a like unfathomable vein,Lao Tzu writes: "The ancient Masters were profound and subtle. Their wisdom was unfathomable. There is no way to describe it; all we can describe is their appearance." (Poem 15) See too in this recondite regard Poems 49 and 67.

5. Here, I'm reminded of this not-so-old joke: People have two great fears, death and speaking in public, and most, if they had to choose between them, would opt for death…

6. Nor is this view peculiar to Lao Tzu. We find it echoed by certain ancient philosophers, e.g., Parmenides, Plato, and the Stoics, by certain religious traditions, e.g., Hinduism, Mahayana Buddhism, and Christianity, and even by certain branches of science, e.g., quantum physics, Unified Field Theory, and holographic theory.

7. And when "the law… [is] written in their hearts," (Poem 32), that is, when they no longer look to religion, morality, or human law for guidance, people will "then trust their natural responses; and everything will fall into place." (Poem 23)

Index

R

S

T

U

W

Y

Z